slow cooking

slow
cooking

EASY SLOW COOKER RECIPES

Katie Bishop

Collins

HarperCollins Publishers

77–85 Fulham Palace Road
London W6 8JB

www.collins.co.uk

Collins® is a registered trademark of
HarperCollins Publishers Limited

First published 2008 by Collins

Text © Katie Bishop, 2008
Photographs © David Munns, 2008

12 11 10 09 08
9 8 7 6 5 4 3 2 1

A catalogue record for this book is available from
the British Library

ISBN-13 978-0-00-728823-6

Colour reproduction by Litho Coloursystems Ltd, London
Printed and bound by Martins The Printers, Berwick Upon Tweed

The publishers and author would like to thank Crock-Pot®
for the use of their slow cookers in the writing of this book.

CONTENTS

INTRODUCTION

Slow cooking is back! Its retro image is being replaced by one of practicality and simplicity in a demanding world where we're all working harder, but wanting to relax and play hard too. Slow cooking allows for both – while the food cooks people are out getting on with their lives and it is ready and waiting to be served to guests or family on their return.

This book is intended to complement a busy lifestyle, providing ideas for slow-cooked food for busy people. Each chapter is intended to suit a different part of the day or a particular occasion, whether it is a work morning breakfast or a weekend brunch, a weeknight supper or romantic meal for two, a dinner party or a relaxed meal for a gathering of friends. All the recipes have been written with the time-conscious in mind, for those who like good-quality (and that doesn't mean expensive!), great tasting food, but may not necessarily have hours in which to prepare it. There are also recipes for those with the inclination to do a little more advance preparation, and those who would rather throw it all into a pot and forget about it! Either way, as working late and/or lengthy socialising become the norm, you can feel confident that slow-cooked food can, in the majority of cases, be left happily for longer than the designated cooking time without spoiling, overcooking or burning.

Celebrity chefs have also begun to extol the virtues of slow cooking at ultra-low temperatures to create meltingly tender results. However, while chefs are able to use high-tech equipment that reduces to temperatures below 60°C (140°F), at home we are more limited. Home ovens usually have a minimum temperature of 110°C (225°F), Gas mark ¼. In the real world the best way for us to replicate ultra-slow cooking and even basic slow cooking is with the use of a slow cooker.

Home cooks have always emulated restaurants to some extent and increasingly that not only takes the form of cooking methods but also ingredients. With the increased use of slow cooking come those foodstuffs particularly suited to it, such as cuts of meat previously deemed to be slightly 'old fashioned' like shins, hocks, necks and brisket, to name but a few. However, while these trends can take things so far, time and people's lack of it seems to continually win when it comes to getting everyday food onto the table.

Slow cooking turns these undervalued and underused cuts into beautiful tender pieces of meat. These cuts are much more affordable than the ever-popular cuts like rump, fillet and sirloin, and have the added value of using up parts of the carcass that may otherwise have been forgotten. Using as much of the animal as possible is good for your wallet, respectful to the animal and critical to farmers' livelihoods.

Slow cookers are also very energy efficient; again allowing you to save money, plus they cook in an environmentally responsible way. Some slow-cooking methods can save up to five times the energy of stove-top cooking since heat is retained rather than being lost to the air, and that has to be a good thing for the planet. Most slow cookers use as little energy as a domestic light bulb. From a practical point of view this also makes cooking more pleasant as the kitchen doesn't steam up and get as hot as it would during conventional cooking. Slow-cooked foods are often redolent of the winter months when stews, casseroles and soups are popular, but the advantage of a cooler kitchen makes slow cooking in the summer just as appealing.

Slow cooking suits the needs of many of us who have little time; it reflects popular trends in the restaurant industry, as well as supporting farmers and making a small contribution to the environment. But, most importantly, slow-cooked food tastes great! Long, gentle cooking allows food to develop flavour in a different way to rapid cooking. It coaxes out flavours that are slower to develop and encourages the flavours of individual ingredients to marry together and blend in a unique way.

Cooking food slowly – it's so 'now'…

Despite being the latest buzzword on the lips of celebrity chefs, slow cooking is far from being a trendy, new phenomenon. Cooking food slowly has been around for as long as we, and our ability to create fire, have. The first stories of humans using fire seem to indicate cooking in large fire pits, where whole animal carcasses would be buried in the midst of slow-burning coals and cooked for 24 hours or more. Stories of similar cooking methods are recounted, and still employed in Australia, by Aboriginal tribes and apparently also in parts of India.

In the late eighteenth century the English scientist Benjamin Thompson is reported to have left a joint of meat in a drying oven overnight, only to be amazed when, the next morning, he found that the meat was tender and fully cooked, although it hadn't browned. He was totally at a loss to explain why this had happened.

Much later, in 1969, Thompson's experiment was repeated by Professor Nicholas Kurti from the University of Oxford during a lecture at the Royal Institution. He showed that the temperature of the meat in Thompson's trial did not go higher than 70°C (158°F), far lower than the temperature at which most of us roast meat, around 200°C (400°F).

In the world wars cooking was frequently done in straw boxes where stews and similar foods were heated over a fire to boiling point and then left encased in a box filled with straw or hay. The food went on cooking, slowly but surely. Wool, feathers, cotton, rice hulls and more recently cardboard, aluminium foil, newspaper, fibreglass, fur and rigid foam have also been documented as good insulators in similar methods now used predominantly by serious campers and explorers.

For many years, Orthodox Jews have been making *cholent* (meaning 'hot food' in Hebrew), a stew simmered over a very low flame or in a slow oven for many hours (up to 24 hours or more) and served on Shabbat (the Sabbath). In some instances the uncooked *cholent* was brought to the local baker before sunset on Fridays and he would put the mixture in his oven, which he always kept fired, and families would come by to pick up their baked *cholent* the next morning.

What's all the fuss about?

Slow cooking achieves three main things – it tenderises (the different proteins in meat are affected by heat at quite low temperatures, far below the heat of a normal roasting oven, between 55–65°C/131–149°F), it flavours (particularly when reaching temperatures around 100°C/212°F), and it kills harmful bacteria (at 68°C/154°F). When meat in particular is cooked for a long time at a low temperature the tough protein, collagen, which holds the muscle fibres together slowly disintegrates and the gelatine that is produced dissolves into any liquid added, which helps to make a rich gravy.

The principle of slow cooking is one of retained heat. In conventional cooking any heat applied to the pot or pan after it reaches boiling point is merely replacing heat lost to the air by the pot. In slow cooking the insulated base and pot prevent most of the heat in the food from escaping into the environment, so little energy is needed to complete the cooking process and moisture is retained in the pot too.

Using a slow cooker

This couldn't be easier – on or off, high or low. In terms of actually using the machine it is very simple.

Some models have a medium setting, which heats up to the cooker's highest temperature and then automatically switches to low for the remainder of the cooking time. Others have a warming function to keep food ticking over at perfect eating temperature after cooking has finished, but that's about as complex as the controls get!

Buying a slow cooker

There are a surprisingly large number of slow cookers available, which vary in size, shape, capacity and price. Prices are surprisingly low in the majority of cases, although as with most things, there is a product to appeal to every consumer and every pocket. As with any kitchen appliance or oven, each brand varies in terms of its heating speed and how evenly it cooks and, as with any oven or appliance, there is an element of getting used to your own model.

Most major brands have a removable inner dish, although some fixed models are available. For flexibility, the removable models are far superior, especially ones that can be used on the hob to sauté – they create less washing up if meat and foods are seared before cooking, and most importantly they retain all the flavours and caramelised loveliness created by sautéing and searing.

Try to buy a model that's suitable for heating in the oven or under a grill – this will give you increased options in terms of finishing dishes to give them colour after cooking. A machine with an in-built digital timer is also a real advantage in terms of ease and convenience and is definitely worth paying a little extra for.

All recipes in this book have been tested in a 5.7 litre (10 pint) family sized cooker. The capacity of your cooker really depends on who and how many you are cooking for, and whether you want to cook large joints of meat, for example, or cakes and puddings. The former are suited to large oval cookers, while a pudding basin or cake tin will need some depth to contain it. A large 5–6 litre (9–10½ pint) cooker is a good all-rounder for this, but it's worth considering its size, especially when it comes to storage. If you are in doubt then go for a larger model than you think you might need as this will serve you well for freezer cooking and entertaining and be more adaptable than one that's simply too small. As a general guide, 1.5–2.5 litre (3–4 pint) cookers are perfect for one and two people, while 2.5 litres (4 pints) will cater for about four. Upwards of 3.5 litres (6 pints) in capacity is perfect for five to six people, entertaining and cooking large batches of food for the freezer.

All slow cookers can be filled to within 2–3cm (^{3}/4–1^1/4in) of the brim, and there is absolutely nothing to worry about when leaving your slow cooker on all day or night without supervision. If you have any worries check your manufacturer's instructions for guidelines on operation times, particularly in terms of the warming function.

Getting organised!

There is no doubt that a slow cooker will save you time and effort in the kitchen. However, to reap the benefits some preparation is required to ensure that you have the right ingredients ready to go before leaving the cooker to do its stuff. Most of this preparation starts with your choice of ingredients.

Choosing suitable ingredients

We have already discussed the increased use of slow-cooked, old-fashioned cuts of **meat** (see page 8). Some cuts (usually forequarter cuts from the front of the animal, or those parts of the animal that have had to work hard, such as legs and necks) are higher in fat and are naturally tougher through more rigorous or regular use. Slow moist cooking enables the protein in these muscles to break down, and produce gelatine, which makes the meat more tender and succulent. A fillet or breast with significantly less fat content may naturally be more tender, as it has done very little while the animal was alive, but will dry out more quickly during slow cooking and have less flavour and an unappealing, dry texture. If using higher fat meat concerns you, then rest assured that in the writing of this book, slow cooking has in the main proved to be a lower fat option to conventional cooking, as searing and frying of ingredients have often been unnecessary. Most meats look and taste better if 'sealed' or browned prior to cooking. However, the notion that meat *must* be browned to 'seal' in the meat juices during cooking and keep it moist is a myth. At 60°C (140°F) meat fibres begin to shrink and release their juice, whether 'sealed' or not. So, unless it is absolutely necessary for taste or appearance, the meat in this book is used directly to save time.

Fruit and vegetables vary too, some being rather more resilient to long slow cooking than others, despite the more delicate temperatures of the slow cooker. As you would expect, root vegetables will take longer cooking than soft, delicate vegetables like cauliflower and broccoli, although you may be pleasantly surprised by vegetables cooked with their skins on, such as aubergines and courgettes, which one may otherwise expect to disintegrate with lengthy cooking. Unless otherwise stated, place vegetables in the slow cooker dish first then top with the meat, if using, as this will ensure that the vegetables cook evenly and absorb all the tasty meaty juices. Fruit follows a similarly logical path, soft fruit breaking down significantly faster than stone fruit or apples and pears, for example, and fruit in skins holding up remarkably well.

Cut **potatoes** will turn black (oxidise) when in contact with the air, as will cut apples, pears and bananas. These must either be completely immersed in liquid during cooking or coated in lemon juice to prevent this 'oxidisation' from happening.

Dairy and sugar do not like very lengthy slow cooking (upwards of 6 hours) as they become denatured, especially when they are in concentrated form in cakes and desserts. Both seem to caramelise unpleasantly and start to break down. However, a few hours are fine, and if well diluted, in water, for example, there are few issues. If in doubt, stir dairy products in at the end of cooking to finish a dish, rather than cook with them for the duration.

Pasta can be cooked in the slow cooker but will become unpleasantly soft if cooked for too long. Try adding pasta to slow-cooked sauces about 30 minutes before the end of cooking. Lasagne and cannelloni are, however, more successful in the slow cooker (see Red Pepper, Basil and Ricotta Cannelloni on page 56).

Rice will absorb lots of excess moisture produced during slow cooking and therefore lots of flavour too. Add about 30–50 minutes before the end of cooking and stir a couple of times to ensure that it cooks evenly.

Dried beans still need to be soaked overnight before being cooked in the slow cooker. Dried red kidney beans must also be boiled for at least 10 minutes before draining and cooking to remove their dangerous toxins. Lentils, split peas and drained, tinned beans can be used directly.

Frozen ingredients must be defrosted before use in the slow cooker, otherwise they are unlikely to reach a safe cooking temperature, making them food poisoning time bombs!

The **cooking liquid** is an important part of success in slow cooking. As water is not lost in slow cooking in the way it is during extended stove-top simmering, the amount of water used to cook foods is normally reduced by about a quarter. Evaporation is reduced in the slow cooker as all the steam is retained in the pot; however, there is still some evaporation as the moisture/steam hits the hot sides of the cooking dish – this again will vary from one machine to another so keep an eye out when you are getting to know your cooker. Use water, stocks, wine, beer, cider, fruit juice or similar to cook in and add flavour. Bear in mind that when cooking with wine or vinegar the lack of evaporation means that the acidity and alcohol doesn't cook off in the same way as stove-top cooking, so the flavour usually remains very pungent and undeveloped.

While cooking in liquid is particularly useful in slow cooking, so too is the ability to use the slow cooker as a water bath (also called a *bain-marie*). Gone are the hours of checking and worrying about steamers and pans boiling dry – this simply doesn't happen in the slow cooker. A water bath is particularly useful when baking, creating a fantastically light sponge or fluffy custard. It's good too in terms of cooking for long periods of time (clearly a moot point when discussing slow cooking, but in this instance a long period of time is 8–9 hours or perhaps overnight). It seems to provide a very gentle cook so that whether cooking overnight or cooking something that's very delicate like a custard, the water bath produces a great result.

How much preparation do you need?

In many cases your preparation will change according to how and when you are cooking your food. If, for example, you are starting your cooking in the morning so that it cooks while you are at work, ready for your return home, then throwing everything into the slow cooker in the quickest possible time will be essential. See the Afterwork Suppers chapter for lots of simple ideas that can be thrown together quickly and then left to their own devices.

Likewise, making a recipe that will cook overnight will require preparation just before you go to bed. So recipes in this instance are short and sweet in the main, with the odd exception for night owls or those with insomnia!

If you are cooking for a large number of people, making sauces, chutneys and jams, or baking cakes and desserts, then allow slightly more time for preparation prior to cooking, but none of the recipes in this book will extend beyond 30 minutes of preparation time.

Importantly, the slow cooker is versatile enough to make all of these types of cooking possible and give good, reliable and above all consistent results every time.

Cooking in a slow cooker

Slow-cooked food should be left to its own devices, so unless the recipe suggests it, food is best left un-stirred with the lid sealed and undisturbed. As tempting as it may seem, lifting the lid to check on progress will cause the cooker to lose heat and moisture, which can affect the quality of the final dish. This is particularly important in the first hour or so of cooking, as this is the time that the cooker is heating the food to a safe and optimal temperature.

Despite being very economical and transferring a limited amount of heat and energy into the atmosphere, the area immediately around the slow cooker will become hot. So using your antique dining table as a base will not serve you well, potentially causing damage to the surface. Instead use a heatproof surface or worktop.

Food should never be reheated in a slow cooker (although Christmas pudding is safe), as it will not heat to a point where the food becomes safe from harmful bacteria and potential food poisoning bugs. Always reheat slow-cooked foods in a pan on the hob, in the microwave or in the oven. Equally, don't leave food to cool down in the slow cooker, as this will create the perfect conditions for unpleasant bugs to multiply – instead, always remove it to another dish.

Check your manufacturer's instructions, but most slow cookers require at least some liquid in the base of the dish to operate properly. You may spot a couple of recipes in this book where this does not happen – this is because these recipes include ingredients that naturally contain a high level of moisture, or there is a large quantity of ingredients, which will create a lot of additional condensation quickly, and therefore a lot of moisture of their own. In some cases, using this method enables some caramelisation of the ingredients in the slow cooker with great results.

Using a conventional recipe in a slow cooker

Most recipes are adaptable to slow cooking and this book gives a good indication of the different cooking methods that work particularly well, in what proportions and for how long. Areas of difficulty are baking, which is a very precise science and requires, in most cases, a blast of heat to encourage rising or to form a crust. Desserts, fish, pasta and rice can all be cooked in the slow cooker but will start to denature during very long, all-day cooking, so that is best avoided for these ingredients.

Some slow cookers can be used in the oven or under the grill and some (although still relatively few) can be used on a hob. Every slow cooker is different and individual manufacturer's instructions should be followed in each case. The slow cooker dish must always be removed from the outer casing before being put in the oven or under the grill. In most instances the removable dish will be ceramic or earthenware and is breakable if dropped and will chip if given reason to do so. The slow cooker base should *never* be cooked in, or immersed in water for cleaning, but simply wiped clean with a damp cloth.

Above all, this book is intended to be a fresh look at slow cooking, a book for how we live today. It offers some classic dishes and others that you probably never have considered possible in a slow cooker. Enjoy the recipes. They have all been lovingly and very thoroughly tested. As mentioned earlier, do continue to bear in mind that every slow cooker is different and yours may be a different size from that used in this book, so times will vary slightly accordingly. You'll soon get to know and love your machine and be able to adapt all the recipes with ease. Treat your slow cooker well and it will be a faithful companion for many years to come!

BREAKFAST AND BRUNCH

Add a few simple ingredients to your slow cooker just before you turn in for the night and get up to a freshly cooked breakfast.

The recipes in this chapter are cooked overnight or for up to 9 hours.

Overnight porridge

PREPARATION TIME: 1 MINUTE
COOKING TIME: 9–10 HOURS
SERVES 2–3   VEGETARIAN

This is gloriously easy to make and it's wonderfully satisfying to know that you can wake up to a bowl of steaming porridge. Yes, porridge can be made in the microwave in minutes, but generally it boils over leaving a congealed mess that takes ages to clean. This slow cooker method is most definitely the way forward...

125g (4½oz) jumbo rolled oats
A large pinch of salt, or to taste
250ml (9fl oz) cold water

Place the oats and salt in a heatproof bowl that fits inside your slow cooker dish. Pour the cold water over the top, but do not stir.

Place the bowl in the slow cooker dish and carefully pour in enough cold water around the outside to come about one-third of the way up the sides of the bowl.

Cover with the lid and cook on low for 9–10 hours. Stir well and season with more salt to taste. Serve with milk or cream, sugar or golden syrup.

WHAT ABOUT...
a rich and hearty porridge. Use a blend of milk and water instead of just water.

Cherry and almond oatmeal

PREPARATION TIME: 5 MINUTES

COOKING TIME: 6–9 HOURS

SERVES 2   VEGETARIAN

Oatmeal makes a very fine, velvety textured 'porridge'. But if oatmeal is not for you then simply replace with the same volume of rolled oats instead.

5 tbsp oatmeal or jumbo rolled
  oats
300ml (10fl oz) cold water
25g (1oz) caster sugar, or to taste
50g (2oz) dried cherries
2 tbsp toasted flaked almonds,
  to serve

Place the oatmeal or oats and cold water in a heatproof bowl that fits into your slow cooker dish. Do not stir.

Place the bowl in the slow cooker dish and pour in enough cold water around the outside to come about one-third of the way up the sides of the bowl.

Cover with the lid and cook on low overnight or for up to 9 hours.

The next morning or just before you are ready to eat, stir in the sugar and dried cherries. Leave to stand for 5–10 minutes or until the fruit starts to re-hydrate. Top with toasted flaked almonds and serve.

TRY...
this with other dried fruits too, such as ready-to-eat dried apricots or dried blueberries.

Spiced apple compote

PREPARATION TIME: 10 MINUTES

COOKING TIME: 6–8 HOURS

SERVES 6   VEGETARIAN

A simple, uncomplicated recipe, this warming compote is perfect for a chilly winter's morning. It's great on its own, with yogurt or to accompany porridge.

50g (2oz) butter, diced, plus extra
  for greasing
6 Bramley cooking apples, peeled,
  cored and diced
6 eating apples, such as Cox,
  peeled, cored and diced
Finely grated zest and juice of
  2 lemons (preferably unwaxed)

1 cinnamon stick
6 whole cloves
2 bay leaves, broken
A large pinch of freshly grated
  nutmeg
125g (4½oz) golden caster sugar,
  to taste

Butter the inside of the slow cooker dish liberally and add the diced apples. Add the lemon zest and juice, then mix well to coat all the fruit in the lemon juice.

Add the cinnamon, cloves, bay leaves and nutmeg and mix well. Dot the top of the apples with the butter, then cover with the lid and cook on low overnight or for up to 8 hours.

Carefully remove the whole spices, add the sugar to taste and mix well. Leave to stand for 5 minutes, then serve hot or allow to cool.

TRY...
cooking this on the hob. Combine all of the ingredients in a large saucepan and warm over a low heat, stirring occasionally, for 1–2 hours or until reduced and thickened.

Cranberry, walnut and orange granola

PREPARATION TIME: 10 MINUTES

COOKING TIME: 5 HOURS

SERVES 4–6   VEGETARIAN

Now, you could cook this faster in the oven, but the slow cooker process seems to enhance the flavour and 'crunch' of this granola. It also means you don't have to check it every 2 minutes to make sure it's not burning. This recipe isn't cooked overnight as others in this chapter are, but it is very easy to make, wonderfully tasty and you know exactly what's gone into it.

200g (7oz) jumbo rolled oats

50g (2oz) walnut pieces

4 tbsp clear honey

Finely grated zest and juice of
 1 orange

2 tbsp caster sugar

A large pinch of ground cinnamon

50g (2oz) dried cranberries

Place the oats and walnuts in the slow cooker dish. Warm the honey, orange zest and juice, sugar and cinnamon together in a small pan over a medium heat for 1 minute or until melted and combined. Pour over the oats and mix well to coat evenly.

Do not cover the slow cooker but turn on to high and cook for 1 hour, stirring occasionally.

Cover with the lid, reduce to low and cook for a further 4 hours, stirring each hour, until crisp.

Tip the mixture out onto a cold baking tray and sprinkle with the cranberries. Leave until cold, then use immediately or keep in an airtight container until needed. The granola will keep for up to a month.

WHAT ABOUT...

if you want to use the oven? Mix the ingredients together as in step 1, then spread out on a baking sheet and cook in an oven preheated to 190°C (375°F), Gas mark 5 for 20–30 minutes, stirring every few minutes or so to prevent it burning.

Apricots with vanilla

PREPARATION TIME: 10 MINUTES
COOKING TIME: 6–9 HOURS
SERVES 4   VEGETARIAN

These delicate, velvety little fruits always seem to disappoint when eaten raw. Slow cooking them coaxes out their unique flavour making them utterly irresistible. Check that your slow cooker is happy on the warming function overnight – read the manufacturer's instructions.

10 fresh apricots, halved and
  stoned
2 lemons (preferably unwaxed)
225g (8oz) caster sugar
1 vanilla pod

Place the apricots in the slow cooker dish. Peel the lemons with a vegetable peeler and add the peel to the apricots together with the juice of half a lemon. Mix gently until the fruit is completely coated in the juice, then pour in enough cold water to cover and add the sugar.

Using a small sharp knife, cut the vanilla pod in half lengthways and scrape the seeds out with a knife into the slow cooker, then add the pod.

Cover with the lid and cook on the warming function overnight or for up to 9 hours until the apricots are meltingly soft. Serve hot just as they are with a little of the syrup, or with muesli and yogurt.

WHAT ABOUT...
making a syrup. Remove the apricots after cooking and pour the syrup into a small saucepan. Bring to the boil over a high heat and simmer for 10 minutes or until reduced and thickened. Spoon the syrup over the apricots and serve.

Overnight yogurt

PREPARATION TIME: 5 MINUTES

COOKING TIME: 6–9 HOURS

MAKES ABOUT 1 LITRE (1¾ PINTS)   VEGETARIAN

It's definitely easier to buy a pot of ready-to-eat yogurt than to make your own. But if you've got lots of milk that needs using up, or you're feeling creative, then why not give this a try. Before trying this recipe, make sure your slow cooker is happy being kept on the warming function for several hours – check your manufacturer's instructions.

2 litres (3½ pints) whole milk
350ml (12fl oz) double cream
200ml (7fl oz) live bio natural
  yogurt

Bring the milk to the boil in a large pan over a high heat. As soon as it boils lower the heat and simmer for 10 minutes or until reduced by a third.

Pour the milk into the slow cooker dish and mix in the cream. Leave for 10 minutes, uncovered, until just lukewarm, then add the yogurt and mix in well.

Cover with the lid and cook on the warming function overnight or for up to 9 hours until thickened.

Spoon the yogurt into a bowl and allow to cool before eating with fresh fruit and muesli. Keep any remaining yogurt covered in the fridge for up to five days.

TRY...
blending the cooked and cooled yogurt with sweetened fruit purée to create your own flavoured yogurt.

Savoury baked ricotta

PREPARATION TIME: 10 MINUTES
COOKING TIME: 6–9 HOURS
SERVES 4–6

A lighter alternative to a full-blown cooked breakfast, this dish is inspired by Aussie breakfast menus where you will see lots of sweet and savoury baked ricotta on offer. This cheesy version is great with grilled tomatoes and crispy bacon, or for something different, try with grilled figs and crispy bacon.

Butter, for greasing
500g (1lb 2oz) ricotta cheese
2 medium eggs
2 tbsp cornflour

75g (3oz) finely grated freshly Parmesan cheese
Sea salt and freshly ground black pepper

Butter a 450g (1lb) non-stick loaf tin and line the base with parchment paper. Place a trivet, up-turned heatproof saucer or cushion of scrunched-up foil into the base of the slow cooker dish.

Place the ricotta in a large bowl and whisk until smooth. Add the eggs, cornflour and Parmesan and beat to combine. Season with plenty of salt and pepper.

Pour the mixture into the prepared tin and level the surface. Place a rectangle of parchment paper over the top, then wrap the tin tightly in greased foil. Place the tin on top of the trivet in the slow cooker, then pour in enough cold water around the outside to just cover the trivet.

Cook on low overnight or for up to 9 hours until firm. Remove the tin from the slow cooker and unwrap. Allow to cool for at least 15–30 minutes before turning out onto a serving plate or board. Using a serrated knife, cut into thick slices and serve topped with grilled cherry tomatoes or figs and crispy bacon.

WHAT ABOUT...
if you want to use the oven? Cook in an oven preheated to 180°C (350°F), Gas mark 4 for 45–50 minutes until just firm.

Hot blueberry and pear Bircher

PREPARATION TIME: 5 MINUTES
COOKING TIME: 6–9 HOURS
SERVES 2   VEGETARIAN

This is a fabulous combination of flavours. Make sure your slow cooker is happy being left on the warming function overnight before you make this – check the manufacturer's instructions.

4 tbsp jumbo rolled oats
100ml (3½fl oz) milk
100ml (3½fl oz) cold water
1 small cinnamon stick

1 ripe pear
100g (3½oz) blueberries
Toasted chopped hazelnuts, for
  sprinkling

Place the oats in a heatproof bowl that fits into your slow cooker dish. Add the milk, cold water and cinnamon stick. Do not stir.

Place the bowl in the slow cooker dish, then pour in enough cold water around the outside to come about one-third of the way up the sides of the bowl. Cover with the lid and cook on the warming function overnight or for up to 9 hours.

When you are ready to eat, coarsely grate the unpeeled pear into the mixture, avoiding and discarding the core. Add the blueberries and fold through to combine. Spoon into bowls, sprinkle with some toasted chopped hazelnuts and serve.

TRY…
making this with whatever fruit is in season. It's great with fresh raspberries and chopped pistachios in the summer.

Spelt and apple bread

PREPARATION TIME: 20 MINUTES
COOKING TIME: 6–9 HOURS
MAKES 1 LARGE LOAF   VEGETARIAN

Spelt has become rather a fashionable ingredient recently and spelt flour is now widely available in supermarkets.

2 tbsp vegetable or sunflower oil, plus extra for oiling
300ml (10fl oz) warm water
50ml (1¾fl oz) apple juice, warmed
1 tsp dried yeast (not fast-action dried yeast)

1 eating apple, cored and grated
Juice of 1 lemon
500–650g (1lb 2oz–1lb 7oz) spelt flour, plus extra for dusting
1 tsp sea salt

Oil a deep non-stick 1kg (2¼lb) loaf tin and place a trivet, up-turned heatproof saucer or cushion of crumpled foil into the base of the slow cooker dish. Pour in enough cold water to come just below the surface of the trivet, about 200ml/7fl oz.

Mix the warm water, apple juice and yeast together in a large bowl and set aside for 10 minutes or until frothy.

Place the apple into a bowl, add the lemon juice and combine. Mix the flour into the yeast mixture, adding a small amount to start with and mixing well between each addition. When the dough begins to come together into a ball, transfer to a floured surface and knead for 5–10 minutes. Continue kneading, gradually adding the salt, vegetable oil and grated apple. Continue kneading for a further 5 minutes or until smooth and elastic.

Place the dough into the prepared tin and cover loosely with a piece of oiled foil, leaving room for the dough to rise, but tightly sealed around the edges. Place on top of the trivet, saucer or foil, in the slow cooker, cover with the lid and cook on low overnight or for up to 9 hours until firm to the touch.

Remove the tin from the slow cooker and allow to rest for 5 minutes. Unwrap and loosen the edges with the tip of a small sharp knife. Turn the bread out onto a wire rack and allow to cool.

Oat, sunflower and honey bread

PREPARATION TIME: 20 MINUTES

COOKING TIME: 6–9 HOURS

MAKES 1 LARGE LOAF · VEGETARIAN

Like rye bread, this is a dense-textured loaf.

2 tbsp vegetable oil, plus extra
  for oiling
1 tbsp dried yeast (not fast-action
  dried yeast)
4 tbsp warm water
250ml (9fl oz) lukewarm milk
50g (2oz) jumbo rolled oats
25g (1oz) oatmeal

1 tsp salt
2 tbsp clear honey
1 egg, beaten
25g (1oz) sunflower seeds
425g (15oz) white bread flour,
  plus extra for dusting

Lightly oil a large deep, non-stick 1kg (2¼lb) loaf tin and place a trivet, up-turned heatproof saucer or cushion of crumpled foil into the base of the slow cooker dish. Pour in enough cold water to come just below the surface of the trivet, about 200ml/7fl oz.

Place the yeast in a small bowl, add the warm water and set aside for 10 minutes or until frothy. Place the oil, milk, oats, oatmeal, salt, honey, egg and half of the sunflower seeds into a mixing bowl and whisk to combine. Add the frothy yeast mixture, then sift in the flour and mix until smooth.

Turn the dough out onto a well-floured surface and knead for at least 5–10 minutes or until smooth and elastic, adding more flour as you need it. Roll the dough into a cylinder the same length as the prepared tin and place smooth side up into the tin.

Sprinkle the remaining sunflower seeds over the top of the dough and cover with a large piece of oiled foil, leaving plenty of space for the loaf to rise, but very tightly sealed around the edges.

Place the tin on top of the trivet or foil in the slow cooker, cover with the lid and cook on low overnight or for up to 9 hours. Remove the tin from the slow cooker and allow to cool for 5 minutes before turning out.

Coconut bread

PREPARATION TIME: 10 MINUTES

COOKING TIME: 6–9 HOURS

MAKES 1 LARGE LOAF   VEGETARIAN

If you don't like coconut don't even think about making this recipe! This is definitely a sweet 'bread', not a cake. It's best cut into slices and then toasted.

75g (3oz) unsalted butter, melted and cooled, plus extra for greasing

2 eggs

300ml (10fl oz) milk

375g (13oz) plain flour

2 tsp baking powder

250g (9oz) golden caster sugar

150g (5oz) desiccated coconut

Butter a large deep non-stick 1kg (2¼lb) loaf tin and line the base with parchment paper. Place a trivet or up-turned heatproof saucer into the base of the slow cooker dish. Lightly whisk the eggs and milk together in a bowl and set aside.

Sift the flour and baking powder into a large mixing bowl. Add the sugar and coconut and mix well. Gradually stir in the egg mixture until just combined; don't worry if there are some lumps, it's better not to overmix as this will make the loaf tough. Fold in the cooled melted butter until just blended. Don't worry about any lumps. Pour the mixture into the prepared tin and cover with a piece of buttered foil, making a pleat in the centre as you go to allow the loaf to rise. Tie tightly with string to seal it completely.

Place the tin on top of the trivet or saucer in the slow cooker and pour in enough cold water around the outside to just cover the trivet. Cover with the lid and cook on low overnight or for up to 9 hours until the loaf is springy to the touch.

Remove the tin and leave to stand for 5 minutes before unwrapping and turning out (you may need to loosen the edges with a sharp knife first) onto a wire rack to cool for at least 30 minutes. Using a serrated knife, cut into thick slices. Toast and serve with cream cheese and Apricot and Cardamom Jam (see page 155).

Oat and blackberry loaf

PREPARATION TIME: 20 MINUTES

COOKING TIME: 6–9 HOURS

MAKES 1 LOAF   VEGETARIAN

This moist flavoursome loaf is not dissimilar to a muffin mixture in texture and taste. It freezes well too – try wrapping individual slices and removing from the freezer as you need them.

150g (5oz) unsalted butter, softened, plus extra for greasing

100g (3½oz) jumbo rolled oats

300ml (10fl oz) boiling water

100g (3½oz) dark brown soft sugar

75g (3oz) caster sugar

2 eggs, lightly beaten

1 tsp vanilla extract

175g (6oz) self-raising flour

A pinch of sea salt

75g (3oz) fresh blackberries

Butter a deep non-stick 1kg (2¼lb) loaf tin and line the base with parchment paper. Place a trivet, up-turned heatproof saucer or cushion of crumpled foil into the base of the slow cooker dish. Place the oats in a heatproof bowl and cover with the boiling water. Set aside until just warm.

In a large mixing bowl, cream the butter and sugars together with an electric mixer until pale and fluffy. Gradually add the eggs, mixing well between each addition, then mix in the vanilla extract.

Sift the flour and salt into the bowl and mix well to combine. Add the oat mixture and fold in to make a batter. Spoon into the prepared tin and level the surface. Dot the top with the blackberries.

Cover with a piece of buttered foil, leaving enough room for the mixture to rise, but well sealed around the edges. Place the tin on top of the trivet, saucer or foil in the slow cooker and pour in enough cold water around the outside to just cover the trivet. Cover with the lid and cook on low overnight or for up to 9 hours until a skewer inserted into the centre comes out clean.

Remove the tin from the slow cooker and allow to cool for at least 20 minutes before turning out, blackberries uppermost, onto a serving plate.

Slow-roasted tomatoes on toast

PREPARATION TIME: 5 MINUTES
COOKING TIME: 6–9 HOURS
SERVES 4   VEGETARIAN

Slowly cooking tomatoes with salt slightly dehydrates them and concentrates their flavour. So if you start with good-quality, great-tasting plum tomatoes and cook them overnight in the slow cooker with salt, they'll taste even better. They are lovely served on toast or as an accompaniment to a full cooked breakfast.

8 plum tomatoes
A large pinch of sea salt
1 tsp caster sugar
1 tbsp balsamic vinegar

Using a sharp knife, cut the tomatoes in half and place them cut side down in a single layer in the slow cooker dish.

Sprinkle over the salt, sugar and vinegar. Cover with the lid and cook on low overnight or for up to 9 hours.

Using a spatula, remove the tomatoes from the slow cooker dish and serve on hot buttered toast.

WHAT ABOUT...

if you want to use the oven? Place the ingredients in a roasting tin and cook in an oven preheated to 110°C (225°F), Gas mark ¼ overnight or for up to 9 hours until the tomatoes are softened and starting to dry out slightly.

Mixed mushrooms on toast

PREPARATION TIME: 5 MINUTES
COOKING TIME: 6–9 HOURS
SERVES 4   VEGETARIAN

While you could certainly fry these ingredients together quickly and create a very tasty dish, slow cooking them encourages the mushrooms to gradually absorb the flavours of the other ingredients, giving them greater intensity and making them utterly more-ish!

500g (1lb 2oz) mixed mushrooms, such as button, cup or portobello, cut into large wedges or thickly sliced
50g (2oz) chilled butter, cubed
2 tbsp olive oil

Sea salt and freshly ground black pepper
Finely grated zest and juice of 1 lemon (preferably unwaxed)
2 tbsp coarsely chopped fresh parsley

Place the mushrooms in a heatproof bowl just large enough to hold them and make sure the bowl fits into your slow cooker dish. Add the butter, olive oil, 1 tsp salt and the lemon zest and juice and, using your hands, mix everything together well.

Place the bowl in the slow cooker dish and pour in enough cold water around the outside to come about one-third of the way up the sides of the bowl. Cover with the lid and cook on low overnight or for up to 9 hours.

Stir well and add the parsley, then season to taste with salt and pepper. Spoon onto hot buttered toast or English muffins and sprinkle with more parsley to garnish. Great topped with a poached egg.

TRY...
using any leftover mushrooms in salads or to make a fantastically flavoursome risotto.

Home-made baked beans

PREPARATION TIME: 5 MINUTES, PLUS SOAKING
COOKING TIME: 6–9 HOURS
SERVES 4 WITH TOAST   VEGETARIAN

You could open a can of course, but this home-made version will leave you wondering why you did! Slow cooking creates an intense depth of flavour and sweetness in this dish, making it taste rich, wholesome and satisfying.

150g (5oz) dried haricot beans
1 x 400g (14oz) tin chopped
  tomatoes
2 tbsp sun-dried tomato paste
2 tbsp tomato ketchup

2 tsp golden caster sugar
300ml (10fl oz) cold water
Sea salt and freshly ground black
  pepper

Place the beans in a bowl and cover completely with cold water. Leave to soak for at least 6–10 hours. Drain and rinse thoroughly and place in the slow cooker dish.

Add the tomatoes, tomato paste, tomato ketchup and sugar, then mix in the cold water. Don't be tempted to season the beans at this point, as the salt will toughen them as they cook.

Cover with the lid and cook on low overnight or for at least 8–9 hours until the beans are tender and the sauce has thickened. Season to taste with salt and pepper and serve spooned over thick hot buttered toast.

TRY...
making this dish with butter beans instead.

Breakfast omelette

PREPARATION TIME: 5 MINUTES
COOKING TIME: 6–9 HOURS
SERVES 6

This recipe caters for a larger number, so making breakfast for a crowd is a doddle.

50g (2oz) butter, diced and softened

650g (1lb 7oz) potatoes, such as King Edward or Maris Piper, unpeeled and diced into 1cm (½in) cubes

12 rashers smoked back bacon, diced

1 onion, peeled and diced

12 eggs

250ml (9fl oz) skimmed milk

½ tsp mustard powder

Sea salt and freshly ground black pepper

Butter the inside of the slow cooker dish very thoroughly with about one-third of the butter, then arrange a layer of the diced potatoes in the base of the dish.

Working quickly so that the potatoes don't have a chance to turn brown, cover the potatoes with a layer of bacon and a layer of onion.

In a large mixing bowl, whisk the eggs, milk and mustard powder together. Season to taste with salt and pepper and pour the mixture into the slow cooker dish. Dot the remaining butter over the top.

Cover with the lid and cook on low overnight or for up to 9 hours until set in the centre.

Remove from the slow cooker base and leave to stand for 5 minutes before cutting into wedges or squares and serving with plenty of crusty bread and grilled cherry tomatoes.

WHAT ABOUT...

adding diced black pudding or chorizo when you add the diced bacon.

Baked eggs florentine

PREPARATION TIME: 10 MINUTES
COOKING TIME: 6–8 HOURS
SERVES 6
                                                          VEGETARIAN

A classic brunch and firm favourite, this version is ideal if you have guests to stay for the weekend. It's quick and easy to prepare the night before so you can wake up knowing that everything is ready for a hearty breakfast.

500g (1lb 2oz) fresh baby spinach leaves

Sea salt and freshly ground black pepper

50g (2oz) softened butter

Juice of ½ lemon

4 shallots, peeled and finely diced

A large pinch of freshly grated nutmeg

12 eggs

250ml (9fl oz) milk

½ tsp mustard powder

Cook the spinach in a large pan of salted boiling water for 1–2 minutes or until just wilted. Drain very thoroughly and cool under cold running water. Drain again and squeeze out as much of the water as possible.

Butter the inside of the slow cooker dish with half of the butter. Place the spinach into the dish in an even layer. Sprinkle with the lemon juice, shallots and nutmeg and season well with salt and pepper. Dot with the remaining butter.

Whisk the eggs, milk and mustard powder together in a large bowl and pour over the spinach. Cover with the lid and cook on low overnight or for up to 8 hours. Serve spooned, spinach uppermost, onto hot toasted, buttered English muffins.

WHAT ABOUT...

baking individual portions in buttered ramekins. Divide the ingredients among 6 ramekins, cover with buttered foil and place in the slow cooker dish. Pour in enough cold water to come about one-third of the way up the sides of the dishes, cover with the lid and cook on high for 2–3 hours or until just firm.

Slow-baked sausages and tomatoes

PREPARATION TIME: 10 MINUTES
COOKING TIME: 6–8 HOURS
SERVES 4

Perfect for brunch, this recipe is quick and easy to prepare and looks after itself overnight while you are sleeping. If you're cooking for a larger number just increase the ingredients accordingly.

2 tbsp olive oil

8 thick sausages, such as pork and herb

3 red onions, peeled and sliced

2 beef tomatoes, thickly sliced

1 fresh rosemary sprig

1 fresh thyme sprig

Sea salt and freshly ground black pepper

Warm half of the olive oil in a frying pan over a high heat. When hot, add the sausages and cook for 5–10 minutes or until well browned.

Place the onions in the slow cooker dish, then drizzle with the remaining oil and toss well to combine. Arrange the tomatoes in a single layer over the onions, then add the herbs and plenty of salt and pepper. Top with the sausages.

Cover with the lid and cook on low overnight or for up to 8 hours. Using a slotted spoon, place the sausages on serving plates, then remove the herbs and discard. Spoon the vegetables onto the plates and serve immediately with plenty of fresh bread to mop up the juices and maybe a fried egg or two.

WHAT ABOUT...

if you want to use the oven? Simply place all of the ingredients into a large roasting tin. Bake, uncovered, in an oven preheated to 180°C (350°F), Gas mark 4 for 60–90 minutes or until browned and caramelised. Turn the sausages occasionally during cooking.

Potato and black pudding hash

PREPARATION TIME: 10 MINUTES
COOKING TIME: 8–9 HOURS
SERVES 6

Not the lowest calorie breakfast but so, so good. It is absolutely perfect for a morning after the night before brunch – or come to think of it, perfect at any time of the day or night!

50g (2oz) chilled butter, cubed, plus extra for greasing
650g (1lb 7oz) potatoes, such as King Edward or Maris Piper, peeled and coarsely grated
1 onion, peeled and diced
250g (9oz) black pudding, cut into 2cm (¾in) pieces
100g (3½oz) grated mature Cheddar cheese
Freshly ground black pepper

Butter the inside of the slow cooker dish very thoroughly. Arrange half of the potato in a single layer over the base of the slow cooker dish, then sprinkle over half of the onion, half of the black pudding, half of the cubed butter and then the cheese.

Repeat this process again, making sure that all of the potato is covered, and ending with a layer of cheese. Season with pepper. Cover with the lid and cook on low overnight or for up to 9 hours.

Serve spooned onto serving plates and top with a poached egg.

TRY...

taking time to make sure that all the potato is covered and not in contact with the air. This will prevent the potatoes from oxidising and turning an ugly grey colour.

Huevos revueltos

PREPARATION TIME: 10 MINUTES
COOKING TIME: 6–9 HOURS
SERVES 4   VEGETARIAN

This version of the classic Mexican scrambled egg breakfast dish is wonderfully flavoursome due to the long slow cooking of the vegetables overnight.

2 plum tomatoes
1 red onion, peeled and diced
2 red peppers, deseeded and diced
1 fresh red chilli, deseeded and finely chopped
2 tbsp olive oil

Sea salt and freshly ground black pepper
10 eggs
25g (1oz) butter
1 tbsp roughly chopped fresh parsley

Place the tomatoes in a heatproof bowl, cover with freshly boiled water and leave to stand for 2 minutes, then drain. Peel the tomatoes, then remove the seeds and cut the flesh into chunks.

Place the tomatoes, onion, peppers, chilli and olive oil in the slow cooker dish and season generously with salt and pepper. Cover with the lid and cook on low overnight or for up to 9 hours until tender and caramelised. Strain off any cooking liquid.

When you wake up or 30 minutes before you are ready to eat, increase the temperature of the slow cooker to high. After 20 minutes, break the eggs into a bowl and whisk lightly, then season with salt and pepper.

Add the egg mixture and butter to the slow cooker dish and stir very gently with a wooden spoon, almost pushing the ingredients lightly, until the eggs begin to set around the edges.

Cover with the lid again and continue cooking for 15 minutes, giving the ingredients a little push every so often, until the eggs just start to become firm. Scatter the parsley over the eggs and spoon onto hot buttered toast to serve.

Overnight bacon and eggs

PREPARATION TIME: 5 MINUTES

COOKING TIME: 6–9 HOURS

SERVES 8–10

Use smoked or unsmoked bacon for this recipe, whichever you prefer. Either way this recipe is a simple solution to cooking breakfast for a larger number.

About 2–3kg (4lb 7oz–7lb) bacon joint (depending on the size of your slow cooker)
1 fresh thyme sprig

4 bay leaves, broken in half
½ tsp black peppercorns
1–2 eggs per person

Place the bacon in the slow cooker dish and pour in enough cold water to cover completely. Drop the thyme, bay leaves and peppercorns into the water. Cover with the lid and cook on low overnight or for up to 9 hours.

The next morning or 30–40 minutes before you are ready to eat, lift the bacon out of the water and set aside in a warm place to rest. Increase the temperature of the slow cooker to high. Gently lower the eggs into the water and leave for 20 minutes for a soft yolk, or for up to 30 minutes for a harder boiled egg.

Remove the eggs with a slotted spoon and leave to stand. When they are just cool enough to handle, carefully peel them. Carve the bacon into thick slices and arrange on serving plates. Top each with an egg or two and cut them in half to expose the runny yolk. Serve with plenty of hot buttered toast.

WHAT ABOUT...

if you want to cook on the hob? Place the bacon in a large saucepan, cover with cold water and add the spices. Bring to a simmer over a low heat and cook for 2–3 hours or until tender. Remove the bacon and increase the heat. When the water is boiling, add the eggs and cook for 5–10 minutes for soft- or hard-boiled eggs, respectively.

EASY LUNCHES

Wake up in the morning and assemble a few ingredients knowing that the slow cooker will have cooked them to perfection by lunch time.

A meal in 2–3 hours.

Creamy beetroot soup

PREPARATION TIME: 15 MINUTES

COOKING TIME: 4 HOURS

SERVES 4   VEGETARIAN

Beetroot makes a great soup, but when it's slow cooked first it's even better! Serve with crusty bread.

4 fresh raw beetroot, about 450g
(1lb) in total, peeled and diced

1 potato, about 100g (3½oz),
peeled and diced

1 onion, peeled and diced

1 tsp caraway seeds, plus extra
to serve

1 litre (1¾ pints) hot vegetable
stock, plus extra if needed

Sea salt and freshly ground black
pepper

200ml (7fl oz) crème fraîche

Place the beetroot, potato and onion in the slow cooker dish. Add the caraway seeds, stock and salt and pepper and mix well.

Cover with the lid and cook on high for 4 hours or until the beetroot is completely tender. Pour the mixture into a food processor and blitz until smooth, adding extra hot stock if it is too thick and needs thinning down.

Spoon all but a few spoonfuls of the crème fraîche into the soup and blitz again to combine. Season to taste.

Ladle the soup into individual bowls immediately and eat warm or leave to cool completely and chill before serving. Hot or cold, serve topped with a dollop of the remaining crème fraîche and a few extra caraway seeds sprinkled over.

WHAT ABOUT...
a lighter alternative. Simply omit the crème fraîche.

Butternut and chilli soup

PREPARATION TIME: 10 MINUTES
COOKING TIME: 4 HOURS
SERVES 4   VEGETARIAN

Making this simple soup will easily fit in around your busy lifestyle. Prepare the squash and relax while it cooks and its flavour slowly concentrates and develops. Then when you're ready to eat, simply boil the kettle, make up the stock, blitz it with the squash and you have lunch ready to go!

1 large butternut squash, about
  1kg (2¼ lb), peeled, deseeded
  and cut into chunks
1 large red chilli, deseeded and
  diced
1 red onion, peeled and diced
2 garlic cloves, peeled and diced

Sea salt and freshly ground black
  pepper
1 tbsp olive oil
1 litre (1¾ pints) hot vegetable
  stock
Fresh coriander leaves, to garnish

Place the squash in the slow cooker dish. Reserve 4 small pinches of chilli for the garnish and add the rest to the slow cooker dish together with the onion and garlic. Season generously with salt and pepper and add the olive oil.

Cover with the lid and cook on high for 4 hours or until the squash is very tender. Spoon the mixture into a food processor (you may need to do this in batches) and add the stock. Blitz until smooth and season to taste.

Ladle the soup into warm bowls, dot with a few coriander leaves and sprinkle with the reserved chilli to serve.

TRY...
making a double batch and freezing some soup for a day when you're too busy to cook.

Farmhouse pâté

PREPARATION TIME: 20 MINUTES
COOKING TIME: 3–4 HOURS
MAKES 1KG (2¼LB) TERRINE (ABOUT 10 SLICES)

Try this rustic pâté served with crusty bread and pickles.

12 rashers smoked streaky bacon

400g (14oz) chicken livers, rinsed

500g (1lb 2oz) pork mince

1 tbsp finely chopped fresh parsley

1 tbsp finely chopped fresh thyme leaves

½ tbsp finely chopped fresh sage leaves

2 shallots, peeled and finely diced

Sea salt and freshly ground black pepper

2 tbsp brandy

1 large egg, beaten

Line a non-stick 1kg (2¼lb) loaf tin with 6 bacon rashers, placing them next to each other horizontally so that the ends of the bacon overhang each side of the tin and the base is completely covered.

Roughly chop 3 of the remaining bacon rashers and 300g (10oz) of the chicken livers and place them in a large mixing bowl. Add the mince and mix well with your hands until the mince is very smooth. Mix in the herbs, the shallots, 2 teaspoons of salt, the brandy and egg.

Spoon half of the mixture into the tin and press down into the corners with the back of a spoon. Place the remaining chicken livers in a single layer over the top and season with some salt and pepper. Cover with the remaining mince mixture and press down again. Cut the remaining bacon rashers in half and lay them horizontally across the base of the terrine, then fold the overhanging ends of bacon over the top to seal everything in neatly. Cover tightly with a layer of parchment paper then foil.

Place the tin in the slow cooker and carefully pour enough boiling water around the outside to come halfway up the sides of the tin. Cover with the lid and cook on high for 3–4 hours or until the mixture is firm and the juices run clear when tested with the tip of a knife. Remove the tin from the slow cooker and leave to cool slightly before unwrapping. Drain off any excess fat, then leave to cool completely. Serve in thick slices.

Caramelised sweet and sour sesame shallots with noodles

PREPARATION TIME: 10 MINUTES

COOKING TIME: 2 HOURS

SERVES 4   VEGETARIAN

When onions and shallots are slow cooked they deserve to be a main ingredient in their own right! Here, they are cooked in a sweet and sour sauce until they caramelise and become meltingly tender and full of flavour.

10–12 shallots

100ml (3½fl oz) red wine vinegar

2 tbsp tomato purée

2 tbsp toasted sesame oil

2 tbsp soft dark brown sugar

2 tbsp toasted sesame seeds

Fresh coriander leaves, to garnish

Using a sharp knife, halve the shallots lengthways and then peel – it's much easier doing it this way, rather than peeling them first. Place the shallot halves in the slow cooker dish.

In a measuring jug, mix the wine vinegar, tomato purée, sesame oil and sugar together. Pour over the shallots and mix well to combine. Ensure that the shallots are nestled together in a single layer.

Cover and cook on high for 1 hour before carefully turning the shallots over. Cover again and cook for a further hour or until the shallots are tender and caramelised.

Scatter over the sesame seeds and toss to combine. Garnish with coriander and serve with freshly cooked egg noodles.

WHAT ABOUT...

if you want to use the oven? Place in an ovenproof dish and cook, uncovered, in an oven preheated to 180°C (350°F), Gas mark 4, turning occasionally, for 1–2 hours or until soft and caramelised.

Hot tomato and pepper bruschetta

PREPARATION TIME: 15 MINUTES

COOKING TIME: 2 HOURS

SERVES 4   VEGETARIAN

Tomatoes and peppers respond wonderfully to slow cooking, becoming far more flavoursome and meltingly tender. Try this instead of chilled tomato bruschetta.

2 tbsp olive oil

3 red peppers, deseeded and cut into thin strips

32 baby cherry tomatoes

1 garlic clove, peeled and cut in half lengthways

Sea salt and freshly ground black pepper

8 slices bruschetta or ciabatta

1 tbsp roughly chopped fresh flat leaf parsley

1 tbsp roughly chopped fresh basil leaves

Extra virgin olive oil, for drizzling

Preheat the slow cooker to high. Pour the olive oil into the slow cooker dish but do not insert into the slow cooker base yet.

Add the peppers and cherry tomatoes to the oil. Finely chop one of the pieces of garlic and add this to the peppers. Season generously with salt and pepper. Cover with the lid and insert the dish into the slow cooker base. Cook on high for 2 hours.

About 10 minutes before you are ready to eat, preheat the grill to its highest setting. Toast the bruschetta or ciabatta for 2–3 minutes on each side until golden. Remove from the grill and rub one side of each slice with the cut side of the reserved garlic. Place them on serving plates.

Add the herbs to the pepper and tomato mixture and season to taste. Spoon onto the garlic toast and serve immediately drizzled with extra virgin olive oil. Great with a handful of rocket leaves.

WHAT ABOUT...

tossing the cooked mixture through freshly cooked and drained pasta, or using it cold to top a home-made pizza.

Apricots with Vanilla

Creamy Beetroot Soup *(above)*
Caramelised Sweet and Sour Sesame Shallots with Noodles *(right)*

Squash, Sage and Walnut Risotto *(left)* ● **Rosti-topped Fish Pie** *(above)*

Whole Roast Chinese Chicken with Plums *(above)*
Vietnamese Beef 'Pho' Broth *(right)*

Spiced Lamb Pilaf

Braised chicory with Parmesan

PREPARATION TIME: 5 MINUTES
COOKING TIME: 2 HOURS 5 MINUTES
SERVES 4

Slow cooking chicory makes it really soft. Here, it is topped with Parmesan and cooked until the cheese forms a lovely golden crust.

4 heads chicory

Juice of 1 lemon

25g (1oz) butter, melted

1 tbsp wholegrain mustard

1 tsp golden caster sugar

4 tbsp freshly grated Parmesan
 cheese (optional)

Using a sharp knife, cut the chicory in half lengthways, then cut out the thick white stem and discard.

Place the chicory in a large bowl, pour over the lemon juice and turn the chicory until it is completely coated in the juice. This will stop the chicory going brown. Arrange the chicory in the slow cooker dish in a single layer cut side down and pour any remaining lemon juice over the top.

Mix the melted butter, mustard and sugar together and drizzle over the chicory. Cover with the lid and cook on high for 2 hours.

If your slow cooker dish is flameproof (see manufacturer's instructions), preheat the grill to its highest setting. Carefully turn the chicory halves over and sprinkle with the Parmesan cheese (if not, transfer to a shallow oven dish before grilling). Place under the hot grill for 3–5 minutes or until golden and bubbling. Serve immediately with salad and crusty bread.

WHAT ABOUT...

if you want to use the oven? Place in a ovenproof baking dish, cover with a tight-fitting lid or foil and cook in an oven preheated to 180°C (350°F), Gas mark 4 for 1–2 hours or until tender.

Herby Italian stuffed peppers

PREPARATION TIME: 15 MINUTES
COOKING TIME: 1½–2 HOURS
SERVES 4   VEGETARIAN

Slow cooking peppers makes them taste amazing as they become tender and sweet. In this very easy dish they are filled with tomatoes, herbs and garlic and finished with mini mozzarella to serve.

4 red peppers

4 tbsp finely chopped fresh herbs, such as basil, parsley or mint

3 tbsp olive oil

16 cherry tomatoes, halved

2 plump garlic cloves, peeled and finely sliced

Sea salt and freshly ground black pepper

16 bocconcini or mini mozzarella

Using a sharp knife, halve the peppers by cutting along the centre of the stalk so that each half has a piece of stalk attached to it. Carefully remove the seeds, leaving the stalks intact and arrange the peppers in a single layer in the slow cooker dish.

Mix the herbs and olive oil together and drizzle into the pepper halves. Divide the cherry tomatoes and garlic equally among the peppers and season with salt and pepper.

Cover with the lid and cook on high for 1½–2 hours or until the peppers are wonderfully soft but still holding their shape.

Place the peppers onto individual serving plates or a single platter and drizzle any juices from the dish over the top. Divide the cheese between the peppers and serve immediately with some rocket leaves and plenty of crusty bread to mop up the juices.

WHAT ABOUT...

if you want to use the oven? Place the peppers on a baking tray and cook in an oven preheated to 170°C (325°F), Gas mark 3 for 1–2 hours or until meltingly tender, then continue as above.

Vegetable frittata

PREPARATION TIME: 10 MINUTES
COOKING TIME: 2½–3 HOURS
SERVES 6

A simple fresh vegetable frittata looks wonderfully colourful and is a great way to use up seasonal vegetables in the summer months.

3 peppers (preferably mixed colours), deseeded and cut into chunks

1 medium courgette, trimmed and cut into chunks

1 medium aubergine, trimmed and cut into chunks

1 red onion, peeled and cut into chunks

12 cherry tomatoes

2 garlic cloves, peeled and roughly chopped

12 new potatoes, washed and cut into quarters

3 fresh thyme sprigs

2 tbsp olive oil

Sea salt and freshly ground black pepper

8 eggs

10 tbsp grated Parmesan cheese

Place the peppers, courgette, aubergine and onion in the slow cooker dish and scatter the cherry tomatoes, garlic, new potatoes and thyme over the top.

Drizzle with the olive oil and season generously with salt and pepper. Mix well with a wooden spoon until all the vegetables are coated in the oil. Cover with the lid and cook on high, stirring occasionally, for 1½–2 hours or until tender. Remove the thyme and discard.

Whisk the eggs and half of the Parmesan cheese together in a bowl. Season generously, then pour the mixture over the vegetables. Replace the lid and cook for a further hour or until just set.

Remove from the slow cooker base and sprinkle with the remaining Parmesan cheese. Run a knife around the edge of the frittata to loosen, then leave to cool, uncovered, for 5 minutes before cutting into wedges or squares to serve.

Cauliflower and parsnip royal korma

PREPARATION TIME: 5 MINUTES
COOKING TIME: 2 HOURS
SERVES 4   VEGETARIAN

This is a wonderfully rich and flavoursome vegetarian korma, which becomes 'royal' with the addition of coconut milk in place of yogurt.

1 large onion, peeled and diced
2 tbsp korma curry paste
400ml (14fl oz) can coconut milk
  (preferably organic)
50g (2oz) ground almonds
1 large parsnip, about 300g
  (10oz), peeled, cored and diced
  into 3cm (1¼in) chunks

1 medium cauliflower, cut into
  small florets
Fresh coriander leaves, to garnish

Place the onion in the slow cooker dish, add the curry paste and coconut milk and mix well. Gradually mix in the almonds, then stir in the parsnip and cauliflower.

Cover with the lid and cook on high for 2 hours or until the vegetables are tender.

Tear the coriander into rough pieces and sprinkle over the curry before serving with warm naan bread.

TRY...
This curry is even better when made 24 hours in advance. Keep covered in the fridge, then reheat thoroughly in a saucepan before serving.

Aubergine and cardamom baba ganoush

PREPARATION TIME: 15 MINUTES
COOKING TIME: 2½ HOURS
SERVES 2–3 AS A MAIN COURSE   VEGETARIAN

Baba ganoush is great as a dip with crudités or as part of a more substantial meal with mezze and pitta bread. In this version, cardamom gives the aubergine a sweet and fragrant flavour.

20 cardamom pods

2 tbsp extra virgin olive oil, plus
  extra for drizzling

1 tbsp lemon juice

1 garlic clove, peeled and crushed

Sea salt and freshly ground black
  pepper

2 medium aubergines, about 250g
  (9oz) each, cut in half lengthways

2 tbsp Greek yogurt

Remove the green outer husks of the cardamom pods leaving only the black seeds behind and crush these lightly in a mortar with a pestle.

In a large bowl, mix the olive oil and lemon juice together, then add the crushed cardamom seeds and garlic. Season with salt and pepper and mix well. Add the aubergine halves and toss in the dressing until evenly coated, then place them in the slow cooker dish. Cover with the lid and cook on high for 2½ hours.

Remove the aubergines from the slow cooker dish and leave to cool slightly. When cool enough to handle, scoop the aubergine flesh out of the skins with a spoon and place in a large bowl. Add the yogurt and mix well. Season to taste.

Spoon the mixture into a serving dish and drizzle more olive oil generously over the top. Serve with warm pitta bread and salad as an appetiser or light lunch.

WHAT ABOUT...

if you want to use the oven? Place the aubergines in a baking dish, cover with foil and cook in an oven preheated to 180°C (350°F), Gas mark 4 for 1–2 hours until tender, then continue as above.

Slow-cooked garlic and herb pasta

PREPARATION TIME: 2 MINUTES
COOKING TIME: 2½–3 HOURS
SERVES 4   VEGETARIAN

Slow cooking garlic makes it gloriously sweet in flavour and absolutely perfect in this creamy pasta dish. This is great with a tomato salad.

1 whole head garlic, unpeeled
100ml (3½fl oz) white wine, plus
  extra if needed
8–12 tbsp crème fraîche, or to
  taste
2 tbsp mixed chopped fresh herbs,
  such as mint, parsley and basil

Sea salt and freshly ground black
  pepper
400g (14oz) dried pasta, such as
  farfalle or fusilli

Place the whole garlic in the slow cooker dish and pour over the wine. Cover with the lid and cook on low for 2½–3 hours, adding more wine if it starts to boil dry, until the garlic is soft.

Remove the garlic from the slow cooker and, using a sharp knife, cut the top from the garlic to expose the tips of the cloves. Squeeze out the now softened flesh into a bowl and mash with a fork until smooth.

Add the crème fraîche and herbs together with any juices from the slow cooker and season to taste with salt and pepper. Mix well.

Cook the pasta in a large saucepan of salted boiling water according to the packet instructions or until tender but still firm to the bite (al dente).

Drain the pasta reasonably well leaving a little of the cooking water behind in the pan. Return the drained pasta to the pan, add the garlic sauce and mix to combine, then serve with a tomato salad.

TRY...
roasting another head or two of garlic at the same time and keeping them well wrapped in the fridge for up to two weeks. Try mixing some of the garlic into mayonnaise for sandwiches or to top jacket potatoes, or even blended with cream cheese and used as a dip for crudités or crisps.

Squash, sage and walnut risotto

PREPARATION TIME: 10 MINUTES
COOKING TIME: 2–3½ HOURS
SERVES 4–6   VEGETARIAN

This colourful risotto is made enticingly flavoursome by the slow-roasting of the squash, which concentrates its already sweet and fragrant flesh.

1 butternut squash, about 1kg (2¼lb), peeled, deseeded and cut into 2–3cm (¾–1¼in) cubes
4 large sage leaves, roughly chopped, plus extra to serve
1 red onion, peeled, halved and thinly sliced
2 garlic cloves, peeled and finely chopped
2 tbsp olive oil

Sea salt and freshly ground black pepper
350g (12oz) risotto rice, such as Arborio
75ml (2½fl oz) marsala or sherry
1.3 litres (2¼ pints) vegetable stock, plus extra to serve
50g (2oz) walnut pieces
Freshly grated Parmesan or crumbled goat's cheese, to serve

Place the squash, sage, onion and garlic in the slow cooker dish. Drizzle with the olive oil and season well with salt and pepper. Cover with the lid and cook on high for 1–2 hours, stirring once during cooking if you can, until tender and starting to colour slightly. Add the rice, marsala or sherry and stock and mix in gently being careful not to break up the squash. Reduce the heat to low, cover and cook for a further 1–1½ hours or until the rice is tender but still has a little bite (al dente).

Season to taste and add a splash of hot stock if you like your risotto creamy. Sprinkle with the walnuts and some extra sage. Serve topped with plenty of Parmesan or crumbled goat's cheese and a tomato, red onion and balsamic salad on the side.

WHAT ABOUT...

roasting a double batch of squash and keeping some in the freezer for another risotto. Alternatively, you can blitz the squash with stock to make a delicious soup, or toss through freshly cooked pasta with some mascarpone to make a great sauce.

Red pepper, basil and ricotta cannelloni

PREPARATION TIME: 25 MINUTES

COOKING TIME: 2 HOURS

SERVES 4

Basil makes this cannelloni amazingly fragrant while the ricotta filling helps keep the mixture light and refreshing.

6 red peppers

250g (9oz) ricotta cheese

6–8 tbsp roughly chopped fresh basil

75g (3oz) finely grated fresh Parmesan cheese

Sea salt and freshly ground black pepper

12 dried cannelloni

200ml (7fl oz) milk

2 eggs

Place the peppers under a preheated hot grill and cook for 10 minutes, turning frequently until completely blackened. Transfer to a large bowl, cover with cling film and leave to stand for 10 minutes. When cool, peel off the skin under cold running water, then remove and discard the seeds, stalk and any white membrane. Pat dry with kitchen paper.

Roughly chop the pepper flesh and place in a large mixing bowl. Add the ricotta, basil and one-third of the Parmesan cheese, season to taste with salt and pepper and mix well.

Remove the slow cooker dish from the base and preheat the slow cooker. Using a teaspoon or piping bag, fill the cannelloni with the ricotta mixture and arrange them in the slow cooker dish, in a single layer if possible.

Measure the milk into a jug. Add the eggs and whisk with a fork to combine. Add 25g (1oz) of the remaining Parmesan and mix in well. Season to taste and pour over the pasta. Cover with the lid and place the dish into the slow cooker base. Cook on high for 2 hours or until the pasta is tender. Five minutes before the end of cooking preheat the grill to its highest setting. If your slow cooker dish is flameproof (see manufacturer's instructions), sprinkle the remaining Parmesan over the top and place under the grill for 3–5 minutes or until golden. Serve immediately.

Creamy pancetta and blue cheese risotto

PREPARATION TIME: 10 MINUTES
COOKING TIME: 1¾ HOURS
SERVES 6

Rich and warming but not heavy, this risotto is just as good for a light summer lunch with salad as it is in the middle of winter with hot buttered vegetables.

125g (4½oz) cubed pancetta
1 large onion, peeled and diced
400g (14oz) risotto rice, such as
  Arborio
2 garlic cloves, peeled and finely
  chopped
100ml (3½fl oz) dry white wine
1.3 litres (2¼ pints) hot chicken or

vegetable stock, plus extra if
  needed
2 fresh thyme sprigs, plus extra to
  garnish
100g (3½oz) blue cheese, such as
  Italian dolcelatte
Sea salt and freshly ground black
  pepper

Warm a large frying pan over a medium heat. When hot, add the pancetta and cook for about 30 seconds. Add the onion, reduce the heat and stir-fry for about 5 minutes or until the onion is softened but not coloured.

Increase the heat slightly, then add the rice and mix well until the rice is coated in the bacon fat. Stir in the garlic and wine and cook for a further minute or until the wine has been absorbed by the rice.

Spoon the mixture into the slow cooker dish and add the stock and thyme. Cover with the lid and cook on low for 1½ hours or until all the stock has been absorbed and the rice is tender but still has a little bite (al dente).

Add a splash of hot stock if you like your risotto creamy, then crumble the cheese over the risotto, season generously with salt and pepper and stir in roughly. Leave to stand for 2 minutes before serving with rocket leaves and a tomato and onion salad.

WHAT ABOUT...
using a strong goat's cheese instead of the blue cheese.

Hot-smoked salmon and potato bake

PREPARATION TIME: 10 MINUTES
COOKING TIME: 2 HOURS
SERVES 4 AS A LIGHT MAIN COURSE

This gloriously rich and fragrant dish is utterly wonderful. Serve warm as opposed to hot or cold to allow the flavours to be at their best.

500g (1lb 2oz) waxy potatoes, unpeeled and thinly sliced into 5mm (¼in) discs
200g (7oz) hot-smoked salmon fillets, skin removed
3 fresh tarragon sprigs
Finely grated zest of ½ lemon (preferably unwaxed)
Sea salt and freshly ground black pepper
300ml (10fl oz) double cream
200ml (7fl oz) semi-skimmed milk

Arrange one-third of the potatoes in a single layer in the base of a shallow baking dish that is just smaller than your slow cooker dish (this recipe will fit a 1.5 litre/2½ pint oval baking dish).

Flake half of the salmon over the potatoes followed by half of both the tarragon and lemon zest. Season generously with pepper.

Repeat this process once again finishing with a final layer of overlapping potato slices – this is the only layer that will be seen, so it is worth taking a little trouble over it to make it look pretty.

Mix the cream and milk together in a jug, then pour gently and gradually over the potatoes, allowing it to seep down into the depths of the dish between each addition. Ensure that the potato is completely covered in cream, then season the top with a little salt and more pepper. Place the baking dish in the slow cooker dish and carefully pour cold water around the outside to come about halfway up the sides of the baking dish. Cover with the lid and cook on high for 2 hours or until the potatoes are tender.

Preheat the grill to its highest setting. Remove the baking dish from the slow cooker and place it under the grill for 2–3 minutes until the top is golden. Serve immediately with a green salad or some seasonal green vegetables.

Peppered mackerel, new potato and caper salad with lemon dressing

PREPARATION TIME: 10 MINUTES

COOKING TIME: 1 1/2 HOURS

SERVES 2

Slow cooking these ingredients together ensures that their flavours intensify and marry in the most wonderful way.

225g (8oz) baby new potatoes, cut in half lengthways

1 tbsp capers in brine, drained (or use salted capers but rinse and drain very well before use)

1 tbsp extra virgin olive oil

Juice of 1 lemon

200g (7oz) smoked peppered mackerel fillets, skin removed

Sea salt and freshly ground black pepper (optional)

100g (3½oz) mixed salad leaves

Cook the potatoes a saucepan of boiling water for 5 minutes, then drain thoroughly and tip into the slow cooker dish.

Add the capers, olive oil and 2 teaspoons of the lemon juice and mix everything together.

Break the mackerel into large pieces and place on top of the potatoes. Cover with the lid and cook on high for 1½ hours or until the potatoes are tender. Remove the lid and add the remaining lemon juice. Check the seasoning and add salt and pepper, if necessary.

Place the salad leaves on two serving plates and spoon the mackerel and potatoes over the top, drizzle the warm juices over to make a dressing and eat straight away.

WHAT ABOUT...

if you want to use the oven? Place in a baking dish, cover with foil and cook in an oven preheated to 160°C (325°F), Gas mark 3 for 1½ hours or until the potatoes are tender.

Prawn and pumpkin curry

PREPARATION TIME: 10 MINUTES
COOKING TIME: 2–3 HOURS
SERVES 4

Fresh, aromatic and colourful, this curry is easy to make and tastes wonderful.

1 orange-fleshed pumpkin or butternut squash, about 1kg (2¼lb), peeled, deseeded and cut into 2–3cm (¾–1¼in) chunks

3–4 tsp Thai red curry paste (see page 77 or use ready-made)

Juice of 1 lime

1 tbsp demerara sugar

200ml (7fl oz) tinned coconut milk

4 large handfuls of baby spinach leaves, washed

250g (9oz) raw tiger prawns

2 tbsp Thai fish sauce, or to taste

4 spring onions, including their green tops, trimmed and finely sliced

Fresh coriander leaves, to garnish

Lime wedges, to serve

Place the pumpkin in the slow cooker dish together with the Thai paste, lime juice and sugar and mix well. Cover with the lid and cook on high for 2–3 hours, stirring once during cooking if you can, until tender and beginning to caramelise.

Add the coconut milk, spinach and prawns. Cover again and cook for a further 15 minutes or until the prawns are pink and opaque.

Season with the fish sauce to taste, then ladle into warm bowls and scatter over the spring onions and coriander leaves. Serve with lime wedges to squeeze over and freshly cooked jasmine rice.

WHAT ABOUT...
making a laksa-style soup. Add 200ml (7fl oz) hot vegetable stock and some cooked fine rice noodles with the fish sauce.

Spicy seafood chowder

PREPARATION TIME: 10 MINUTES

COOKING TIME: 2¼ HOURS

SERVES 4

A hearty soup with just enough spice to give your taste buds a bit of a kick. If you don't like spicy food, then either add more crème fraîche or simply less chilli.

4 rashers smoked streaky bacon, diced

4 tbsp dry vermouth

1 small onion, peeled and finely diced

2 celery sticks, trimmed and cut into 5mm (¼in) pieces

250g (9oz) floury potatoes, peeled and diced into 1cm (½in) cubes

2 corn on the cob

2 bay leaves, broken

500ml (18fl oz) chicken or vegetable stock

2 red chillies, deseeded and finely diced

3 tbsp crème fraîche

250g (9oz) mixed ready-to-eat, cooked seafood, such as prawns, calamari or mussels

1 tbsp chopped fresh dill

Warm a frying pan over a medium heat. When hot, add the bacon and stir-fry for about 5 minutes or until opaque but not coloured. Add the vermouth and remove the pan from the heat. Stir well, scraping any caramelised bacon from the base of the pan, pour into the slow cooker dish, then add the onion, celery and potatoes to the slow cooker dish.

Stand the corn on their ends and carefully run a knife from top to bottom to cut off the kernels. Add to the slow cooker dish together with the bay leaves and stock.

Place half of the chillies in the slow cooker dish and set the rest aside. Cover with the lid and cook on high for 2 hours or until the potato is tender.

Ladle half of the chowder into a food processor and blitz until smooth. Return the purée to the slow cooker dish and mix in. Add the crème fraîche, seafood and the remaining chillies and mix to combine. Cover again and leave for 15 minutes to heat through thoroughly. Serve immediately in warm bowls, sprinkled with chopped dill.

Rosti-topped fish pie

PREPARATION TIME: 10 MINUTES
COOKING TIME: 3 HOURS
SERVES 4

Fish is usually best cooked very quickly to retain its moist texture. In this instance, cooking the fish in a tasty tomato sauce retains its succulence while allowing its flavours to develop and combine with the sauce to make a fantastic pie.

500g (1lb 2oz) firm white fish fillets, such as cod, haddock or pollack, cut into 4cm (1½in) pieces

200g (7oz) mixed ready-to-eat, cooked seafood, such as prawns, calamari or mussels

1 x 400g (14oz) tin chopped tomatoes

1 tbsp tomato purée

50ml (1¾fl oz) vermouth (optional)

2 tbsp finely chopped fresh dill

1 garlic clove, peeled and crushed

Sea salt and freshly ground black pepper

3–4 large potatoes, about 850g (1lb 14oz) in total

Juice of ½ lemon

50g (2oz) butter, melted and cooled slightly

Place the fish in the slow cooker dish with the seafood.

Add the tomatoes, tomato purée, vermouth (if using), dill and garlic. Season generously with salt and pepper and mix gently to combine.

Peel and coarsely grate the potatoes into a large bowl. Drizzle the lemon juice over and mix well. Pour the melted butter over the top and mix again. Season well and spoon the topping evenly over the tomato mixture until completely covered.

Cover with the lid and cook on low for 3 hours or until the potato is tender.

If your slow cooker dish is flameproof (see manufacturer's instructions), preheat the grill to its highest setting and place the dish under the grill for 5–10 minutes or until golden brown. Serve immediately with peas.

WHAT ABOUT...
Other firm-fleshed fish, such as smoked haddock, work equally well.

Garlic chicken carbonara

PREPARATION TIME: 10 MINUTES
COOKING TIME: 2–3 HOURS
SERVES 4

This is a simple family favourite with the addition of slow-cooked chicken breast. It's great for informal entertaining too.

300g (10oz) boneless chicken breast, about 2 breasts, cut into 2cm (¾in) pieces

100g (3½oz) pancetta, cut into 2cm (¾in) pieces

1 tbsp plain flour

1 garlic clove, peeled and finely chopped

100ml (3½fl oz) white wine

Sea salt and freshly ground black pepper

100ml (3½fl oz) double cream

400g (14oz) dried spaghetti

2 egg yolks, beaten

2 tbsp chopped fresh parsley

Place the chicken and pancetta in the slow cooker dish and sprinkle the flour over the top. Mix well with a wooden spoon until the meat is coated in the flour. Add the garlic and wine and season generously with salt and pepper. Cover with the lid and cook on low for 2–3 hours, stirring every now and again if you're around, until the sauce is thick and no longer tastes floury.

After cooking, remove the slow cooker dish from the heated base and beat in the cream, making sure there are no lumps remaining. Leave to stand for about 5 minutes to cool slightly.

Meanwhile, bring a large pan of salted water to the boil. Add the spaghetti and cook for 10 minutes or until tender but still firm to the bite (al dente). Drain, keeping about 2 tablespoons of the cooking water if you can.

Add the egg yolks to the chicken mixture and mix quickly to combine. Check the seasoning, adding more salt and pepper if necessary.

Tip the cooked pasta and the reserved cooking water into the sauce and mix well. Scatter the chopped parsley over the top and serve immediately on warm plates with a green salad.

Country chicken with tarragon and cream

PREPARATION TIME: 15 MINUTES
COOKING TIME: 2 HOURS
SERVES 4

This hearty, warming stew is true comfort food without being heavy.

1 tbsp olive oil
25g (1oz) butter
4 chicken legs
500g (1lb 2oz) baby new potatoes,
  washed and halved
6 shallots, peeled and halved

150ml (5fl oz) cider
2 large fresh tarragon sprigs,
  leaves only
4 tbsp crème fraîche
Sea salt and freshly ground black
  pepper

Warm the olive oil and butter in a large frying pan over a high heat. When hot, add the chicken legs and cook for about 5 minutes or until evenly browned all over. Place the potatoes in the slow cooker dish and top with the chicken.

Return the pan to the heat, add the shallots and cook, stirring frequently, for 5–10 minutes until golden. Add the cider and allow to bubble ferociously for 30–60 seconds or until it reduces by about half. Add half of the tarragon, then pour over the chicken. Cover with the lid and cook on high for 2 hours.

Using a slotted spoon, place the chicken and potatoes on warm serving plates. Mix the crème fraîche into the sauce, add the remaining tarragon and season to taste with salt and pepper. Spoon over the chicken and serve with a green salad.

TRY...
this dish with chicken thighs or a combination of chicken legs and thighs.

Tandoor-style chicken

PREPARATION TIME: 10 MINUTES, PLUS 3 HOURS MARINATING
COOKING TIME: 3–4 HOURS
SERVES 4

If you use a good-quality tandoori paste for this recipe there's no need to make your own.

8 chicken thighs

125g (4½oz) natural yogurt

3–4 tbsp tandoori paste, to taste

1 garlic clove, peeled and crushed

1 tbsp lime juice

2 tbsp finely chopped fresh mint

Using a sharp knife, slash each chicken thigh three times down to the bone and place in a shallow dish.

Mix the remaining ingredients together in a bowl and spoon over the chicken. Mix well until the chicken is coated in the yogurt mixture. Cover and chill for at least 3 hours or overnight.

The next morning or when you are ready to cook, preheat the slow cooker on high for 30 minutes. Arrange the chicken skin side down in a single layer in the warmed slow cooker dish. Cover with the lid and cook for 3–4 hours or until the chicken is tender and browned. Serve with warm naan bread and salad.

WHAT ABOUT...
coating a whole chicken or baby poussin with the spicy yogurt mixture and cooking in the slow cooker until tender and the juices run clear when the thickest part of the meat is pierced with a skewer.

Chorizo in sherry and tomato sauce

PREPARATION TIME: 10 MINUTES

COOKING TIME: 2½ HOURS

SERVES 4 AS A LIGHT, TAPAS-STYLE LUNCH OR STARTER

This is a wonderful tapas dish or just as good as a starter – try it spooned onto toasted bruschetta.

200g (7oz) chorizo sausage, thickly sliced

2 garlic cloves, peeled and finely sliced

250g (9oz) baby new potatoes, washed and cut into thick slices

Sea salt and freshly ground black pepper

400g (14oz) cherry tomatoes, halved

2 tbsp dry fino sherry

1 tsp caster sugar

2 tbsp roughly chopped fresh flat leaf parsley

Turn the slow cooker on to its highest setting. Place the chorizo and garlic in the slow cooker dish, cover with the lid and leave to cook for 30 minutes or until the chorizo has started to leach its orange, paprika-coloured oil.

Meanwhile, cook the potatoes in a saucepan of salted boiling water over a high heat for 5 minutes or until just becoming tender. Drain and set aside.

Add the cherry tomatoes to the slow cooker dish together with the potatoes, sherry and sugar. Mix well, cover with the lid and leave to cook for a further 2 hours. Season to taste with salt and pepper and mix in the parsley. Serve hot with crusty bread to mop up the sauce.

WHAT ABOUT...

if you want to use the oven? Omit the first step and place the par-boiled potatoes and the other remaining ingredients into a large baking dish, cover with a tight-fitting lid or foil and cook in an oven preheated to 180°C (350°F), Gas mark 4 for 1–2 hours or until the potatoes are tender.

AFTERWORK SUPPERS

Throw some ingredients into the
slow cooker before you leave for work
in the morning and come home
to a delicious hot meal.

A meal in 6 to 9 hours.

Hot gazpacho

PREPARATION TIME: 15 MINUTES

COOKING TIME: 2 HOURS

SERVES 4   VEGETARIAN

It may seem a travesty to warm this usually chilled soup, but do try this version, as the gentle heat of slow cooking gives it a new dimension. This soup is great served with warm cheese straws to dip in.

1 vegetable stock cube

75ml (2½fl oz) boiling water

500g (1lb 2oz) ripe tomatoes

½ small cucumber, peeled and roughly chopped

1 red pepper, deseeded and roughly chopped

2 garlic cloves, peeled and chopped

1 large fresh coriander sprig, roughly chopped

1 tsp light muscovado sugar

Sea salt and freshly ground black pepper

50ml (1¾fl oz) basil-infused extra virgin olive oil (or if unavailable use the same amount of good-quality extra virgin olive oil)

Place the stock cube in a jug and add the boiling water. Mix well to make a very concentrated stock, then pour the stock into the slow cooker dish.

Using a small sharp knife, score the base of each tomato. Place them in a large bowl and cover with boiling water. Leave for 1–2 minutes, then drain and immediately cover in cold water. Remove each tomato and peel – the skins should come away easily. Quarter the tomatoes and, if you have the time and the inclination, remove the seeds – if not don't worry. Add the tomatoes to the slow cooker dish.

Add the cucumber, chopped pepper, garlic and coriander to the slow cooker dish, cover with the lid and cook on low for 2 hours or until the vegetables are very tender.

Transfer the soup to a food processor or blender, in batches if necessary, and blitz until completely smooth. Season with the sugar, and salt and pepper to taste. The soup should still be piping hot so serve immediately in small bowls drizzled liberally with the basil oil.

Beetroot, thyme and goat's cheese salad

PREPARATION TIME: 10 MINUTES

COOKING TIME: 4 HOURS

SERVES 4   VEGETARIAN

Slow cooking beetroot coaxes out its sweetness and flavour. It's particularly good twinned with thyme and goat's cheese in this tasty salad.

1 bunch (about 4) fresh raw
  beetroot, scrubbed
2 garlic cloves, peeled and
  crushed
4 fresh thyme sprigs
2 tbsp balsamic vinegar
2 tbsp extra virgin olive oil

1 tbsp orange juice
2 tbsp redcurrant jelly
Sea salt and freshly ground black
  pepper
150g (5oz) mixed salad leaves
200g (7oz) goat's cheese

Trim the roots and the green leafy tops from the beetroot and set the leaves aside if they are in good condition. Cut the beetroot into quarters and place in the slow cooker dish together with the garlic, thyme, balsamic vinegar, olive oil, orange juice and redcurrant jelly. Season with salt and pepper.

Cover with the lid and cook on low for 4 hours or until the beetroot is wonderfully tender. Remove from the heat and leave to cool in the slow cooker dish.

Place the salad and any reserved beetroot leaves onto individual serving plates, top with the beetroot and drizzle with some of the cooking juices. Crumble the cheese over the top and serve with crusty bread.

TRY...
using blue cheese, Brie or Camembert instead of goat's cheese.

The best and easiest tomato pasta sauce

PREPARATION TIME: 5 MINUTES
COOKING TIME: 8–12 HOURS
SERVES 4   VEGETARIAN

There still seems to be a certain suggestion that tinned food is inferior to fresh. When it comes to cooking with tomatoes, and especially tomato sauce, tinned tomatoes are the way to go!

2 x 400g (14oz) tins chopped tomatoes

1 small onion, peeled and finely diced

2 garlic cloves, peeled and crushed

1 tsp dried oregano

1 tsp sea salt

1 tbsp caster sugar

100ml (3½fl oz) red wine

60ml (2fl oz) extra virgin olive oil

Fresh basil leaves, torn, to garnish

Freshly grated Parmesan cheese, to serve

Place the tomatoes, onion, garlic, oregano, salt, sugar and wine into the slow cooker dish. Drizzle over half of the olive oil and mix well.

Cover with the lid and cook on low for 8 hours or for up to 12 hours.

Season with more salt to taste and mix in the remaining olive oil. Spoon over hot, freshly cooked pasta and sprinkle with torn basil leaves and grated Parmesan to serve.

TRY...

adding a whole dried chilli to the sauce at the start of cooking for an extra kick. Remove it before serving.

Black bean gumbo

PREPARATION TIME: 5 MINUTES, PLUS SOAKING
COOKING TIME: 6–8 HOURS
SERVES 4   VEGETARIAN

This gumbo is spicy in a warming and soothing way, but is definitely hot, so if you like something a little bit milder just add less white pepper.

200g (7oz) dried black beans or black-eyed beans
1 red onion, peeled and finely chopped
2 celery sticks, trimmed and finely chopped
2 garlic cloves, peeled and crushed
2 red chillies, deseeded and finely chopped

150ml (5fl oz) vegetable stock
2 x 400g (14oz) tins chopped tomatoes
1 tsp dried thyme
1 tsp cayenne pepper
1 tsp dried oregano
¼–½ tsp white pepper
½ tsp sea salt
200g (7oz) baby spinach leaves, washed

Soak the beans in a bowl of cold water overnight. The next day, drain and place in the slow cooker dish.

Add the onion and celery to the dish together with the garlic and chillies, then add the remaining ingredients except the salt and spinach and mix well.

Cover with the lid and cook on low for 8 hours. Season to taste with the reserved salt and stir in the spinach just before serving with tortillas or freshly cooked long-grain rice.

WHAT ABOUT...
using other dried beans; but if you use red kidney beans you must soak them overnight and boil according to the packet instructions before use.

Vegetarian shepherd's pie with celeriac and Cheddar topping

PREPARATION TIME: 20 MINUTES
COOKING TIME: 7–9 HOURS
SERVES 6

VEGETARIAN

There is no reason why a meat eater should feel hard done by when eating this shepherd's pie – it just happens to be vegetarian!

1 large red onion, peeled and chopped

2 carrots, peeled and diced

500g (1lb 2oz) parsnips, peeled and diced

200ml (7fl oz) red wine (preferably vegetarian)

1 tbsp chopped fresh rosemary leaves

1 x 400g (14oz) tin chopped tomatoes

200g (7oz) Puy or green lentils, rinsed and drained

250ml (9fl oz) vegetable stock

Sea salt and freshly ground white pepper

For the topping:

850g (1lb 14oz) celeriac, peeled and roughly chopped

350g (12oz) potatoes, peeled and roughly chopped

75g (3oz) grated mature Cheddar cheese

Place all of the ingredients except for the seasoning and the topping in the slow cooker dish. Mix well but do not season at this stage, as salt will toughen the lentils. Cover with the lid and cook on low for 6–8 hours or until thickened.

When you get home from work or 30 minutes before you are ready to eat, cook the celeriac and potato pieces in a large saucepan of boiling water for 10–15 minutes or until tender. Drain thoroughly and return to the pan. Add two-thirds of the cheese and mash well until completely smooth. Season to taste with salt and pepper.

If your slow cooker dish is flameproof (see manufacturer's instructions), preheat the grill to its highest setting. Season the lentil mixture in the slow cooker to taste and spoon the mashed celeriac mixture evenly over the top to cover the lentils completely.

Sprinkle the remaining cheese over the top of the mash and cook under the grill for 5–10 minutes or until golden brown. Allow to cool for about 5 minutes before serving with seasonal green vegetables or salad.

TRY...
spooning the cooked lentil mixture into individual portion freezerproof containers, allowing to cool, then topping with the mash and freezing for those days when cooking is not an option. Reheat from frozen in an oven preheated to 180°C (350°F), Gas mark 4 for 30–40 minutes or until hot.

Red lentil and tomato dhal

PREPARATION TIME: 5 MINUTES
COOKING TIME: 6 HOURS
SERVES 4   VEGETARIAN

This tastes great and is perfect as a side dish to go with curry or on its own with naan bread.

1 red onion, peeled and finely sliced

1 garlic clove, peeled and finely chopped

2 tbsp medium curry paste (choose a milder or hotter one if you prefer)

2 x 400g (14oz) tins chopped tomatoes

250g (9oz) red lentils, rinsed and drained

500ml (18fl oz) vegetable stock

Sea salt

Add the onion and garlic to the slow cooker dish. Mix in all the remaining ingredients and season well with salt.

Cover with the lid and cook on low for 6 hours or until thickened and the lentils are tender and beginning to break down.

Serve topped with spoonfuls of natural yogurt or raita with poppadums or naan bread.

Moroccan chicken with preserved lemons and couscous

PREPARATION TIME: 20 MINUTES
COOKING TIME: 6–8 HOURS
SERVES 4

Do try to get preserved lemons for this, as it makes all the difference. If you can't, simmer a halved fresh lemon for about 8 minutes and use this. Raw lemon will be far too powerful in this dish.

4 chicken legs

Sea salt and freshly ground black pepper

1 tbsp olive oil

25g (1oz) butter

2 large onions, peeled and finely diced

2 garlic cloves, peeled and crushed

1 tsp ground cinnamon

1 tsp ground ginger

4 small preserved lemons, quartered

A handful of black olives, whole or sliced

250g (9oz) couscous

Fresh coriander leaves, for sprinkling

Season the chicken legs with salt and pepper. Warm the olive oil and butter in a large frying pan and, when hot, add the chicken. Cook for about 5 minutes or until golden on both sides. Arrange the chicken in the slow cooker dish in a single layer and pour any cooking juices over the top.

Scatter the onions in a layer over the chicken, then add the garlic and spices. Tuck the preserved lemons between the chicken pieces and pour in enough cold water (about 150ml/5fl oz) to come halfway up the sides of the chicken. Cover with the lid and cook on low for 6–8 hours or until the chicken is tender and the sauce is wonderfully aromatic.

About 15 minutes before eating, remove the chicken from the slow cooker dish and keep warm. Add the olives and couscous to the dish and mix well. Season and cover with the lid again. Leave to steam for 10 minutes or until the couscous is tender but still has a bite (al dente).

Spoon the couscous onto warm serving plates. Top with the chicken, sprinkle with coriander and serve with a green salad.

Whole roast Chinese chicken with plums

PREPARATION TIME: 15 MINUTES
COOKING TIME: 6 HOURS
SERVES 4

Whole roast chicken isn't just for Sunday! Try this great dish – with Chinese five-spice and sherry giving the chicken a delicious Chinese flavour – on any day of the week. This is great served with freshly cooked noodles and steamed pak choi.

1–1.5kg (2¼–3¼lb) free-range chicken
1 tbsp groundnut oil
1 tbsp Chinese five-spice powder
750g (1lb 10oz) just ripe plums (about 8), halved and stoned

75ml (2½ fl oz) dry fino sherry
150ml (5fl oz) vegetable stock
1 tbsp clear honey
Sea salt and freshly ground black pepper

Pat the chicken dry with kitchen paper. Warm the groundnut oil in a large frying pan over a high heat. When hot, add the chicken and sear on all sides until golden brown. Allow to cool slightly, then rub with the five-spice powder.

Place the plums in the slow cooker dish together with the sherry and stock.

Cover with the lid and cook on low for 6 hours. Remove the chicken and set aside in a warm place covered in a tent of foil. Stir the honey into the plum sauce and season to taste with salt and pepper.

Carve the chicken into portions (it will be so tender that you may not need a knife, just a spoon and fork to divide it) and serve with plenty of sauce and plums spooned over.

TRY...
buying a bigger bird so that there is plenty left for a cold lunch the next day.

Sticky orange and sesame chicken drumsticks

PREPARATION TIME: 12 MINUTES
COOKING TIME: 6 HOURS
SERVES 4

These tender pieces of chicken are coated in a glossy glaze that is full of flavour.

8 chicken drumsticks
Finely grated zest and juice of
  1 large orange
2 tbsp dark muscovado sugar
2 tsp Chinese five-spice powder

2 tbsp Japanese teriyaki sauce or
  dark soy sauce
1 tbsp toasted sesame oil
1 tbsp sesame seeds, to garnish

Warm a large non-stick frying pan over a high heat. When hot, add the chicken drumsticks and cook for 10 minutes until golden. Place the chicken in the slow cooker dish.

Sprinkle the orange zest over the chicken and pour in the juice. Add all the remaining ingredients except the sesame seeds and carefully mix everything together until the chicken is coated in the sauce.

Cover with the lid and cook on low for 6 hours or until the chicken is thoroughly cooked and piping hot.

Spoon the chicken onto a large serving plate and scatter the sesame seeds over the top. Serve drizzled with cooking juices with freshly cooked egg noodles or rice and stir-fried vegetables.

WHAT ABOUT...
using chicken wings or thighs, or pork ribs.

Thai chicken with home-made curry paste

PREPARATION TIME: 15 MINUTES
COOKING TIME: 6–9 HOURS
SERVES 4

If you don't have time to create your own curry paste, use a good-quality shop-bought paste instead and use about 2–3 tablespoonfuls. Buy fresh kaffir lime leaves from Asian food stores or freeze-dried from some major supermarkets.

1 x 400ml (14fl oz) tin coconut milk

1 red pepper, deseeded and cut into strips

125g (4½oz) green beans, trimmed and cut into 4cm (1½in) lengths

125g (4½oz) aubergine, trimmed and cut into 2cm (¾in) cubes

4 boneless, skinless chicken breasts

½ tbsp caster sugar, to taste

Thai fish sauce, to taste

Lime juice, to taste

Lime wedges, to serve

For the curry paste:

2 shallots, peeled and chopped

1 lemongrass stalk, peeled and roughly chopped

2 tsp chopped fresh root ginger

1 tsp shredded fresh kaffir lime leaves

2 red bird's eye chillies, deseeded if you like

3 garlic cloves, peeled

½ tsp coriander seeds

½ tsp cumin seeds

2 tbsp Thai fish sauce

A large pinch of turmeric

Place all the curry paste ingredients in a food processor and blitz to make a textured mixture. Spoon the paste into the slow cooker dish and gradually mix in the coconut milk.

Place the vegetables in the slow cooker dish, then add the chicken and mix well to ensure it is immersed in the coconut milk.

Cover with the lid and cook on low for 6–9 hours or until the chicken is tender and the coconut milk has reduced slightly. If the sauce looks as if it has split, don't worry, just give it a good stir. Season with the sugar, fish sauce and lime juice to taste and serve with lime wedges on the side.

Mexican chicken mole with chocolate

PREPARATION TIME: 15 MINUTES
COOKING TIME: 6–8 HOURS
SERVES 4

This gorgeous recipe uses chipotle paste – a smoked chilli paste pronounced 'chip-oat-lay'. Most supermarkets or delicatessens sell it these days. The dark chocolate gives the sauce a glorious richness.

2 tbsp olive oil
½ tsp dried chilli flakes
½ tsp cumin seeds
1 red onion, peeled and diced
2 garlic cloves, peeled and roughly
  chopped
100g (3½oz) ground almonds
1 tsp chipotle (smoked chilli) paste
1 tbsp soft dark brown sugar
¼ tsp sea salt

¼ tsp ground cinnamon
25g (1oz) dark plain chocolate
1 tbsp red wine vinegar
2 tbsp tomato purée
250ml (9fl oz) hot chicken or
  vegetable stock
4 chicken legs
Fresh coriander leaves, to serve

Warm the olive oil in a frying pan over a medium heat. When hot, add the chilli and cumin and stir-fry for 1 minute or until fragrant. Add the onion and garlic and cook for about 4 minutes or until the onion is lightly browned. Remove from the heat and stir in the almonds so that they absorb all the spicy oil.

Spoon the warm onion mixture into a food processor. Add the chipotle, sugar, salt, cinnamon, chocolate, vinegar, tomato purée and about half of the stock and blitz to make a smooth, thick paste.

Spoon the spice paste into the slow cooker dish and add the chicken. Turn the chicken over in the paste to coat completely, then arrange the chicken in a single layer, skin side down, and pour over the remaining stock.

Cover with the lid and cook on low for 6–8 hours or until the chicken is meltingly tender and beginning to caramelise on the base of the dish. Serve with fresh coriander, and dollops of soured cream on the side.

Chunky chilli

PREPARATION TIME: 20 MINUTES
COOKING TIME: 8–9 HOURS
SERVES 8–10

This recipe uses shin of beef. Its rich, unctuous flavour makes it absolutely perfect for slow cooking and it is also ideal for freezing.

900g (2lb) beef shin or braising steak, cut into 1–2cm (½–¾in) pieces
3 tbsp plain flour
1 tbsp cocoa powder
1 large onion, peeled and chopped
2 red chillies, deseeded and chopped
2 garlic cloves, peeled and roughly chopped

2 x 400g (14oz) tins chopped tomatoes
Sea salt and freshly ground black pepper
1 x 410g tin red kidney beans, drained and rinsed
Chopped fresh coriander, to garnish

Place the meat in a large freezer bag together with the flour and cocoa. Seal the bag and toss the contents together until the meat is evenly coated.

Place the meat and any remaining flour and cocoa in the slow cooker dish together with the onion, chillies, garlic and tomatoes. Season generously with salt and pepper and mix well. Cover with the lid and cook on low for at least 8 hours or until thick and the meat is wonderfully tender.

Stir in the kidney beans and cover again and cook for a further 15 minutes or until the beans are piping hot. Garnish with the chopped coriander and serve with freshly cooked rice, shredded iceberg lettuce and spoonfuls of soured cream.

WHAT ABOUT...

if you want to use the oven? Follow the recipe and place into a casserole dish, cover with a tight-fitting lid or foil and cook in an oven preheated to 150°C (300°F), Gas mark 2 for 4–6 hours.

Vietnamese beef 'pho' broth

PREPARATION TIME: 5 MINUTES

COOKING TIME: 8–10 HOURS

SERVES 4

This is a substantial meal in a bowl. It's a nice idea to assemble this dish at the dining table – serve a bowl of noodles and then a selection platter with bean sprouts, spring onions and more sliced chilli for example – and let people customise their own broth.

400g (14oz) beef feather steak (available from good butchers) or braising steak, sliced into thin strips

1 red chilli, sliced

1 tsp shredded fresh root ginger

1 garlic clove, peeled and left whole

6 cloves (optional)

1.3 litres (2¼ pints) cold good-quality beef stock

250g (9oz) vermicelli (fine rice noodles)

100g (3½oz) bean sprouts

4 spring onions, trimmed and finely shredded

4 tbsp roughly chopped coriander leaves, plus some whole

4 tbsp roughly chopped mint leaves, plus some whole

Juice of 1 lime, to taste

1 tbsp fish sauce, to taste

Lime wedges, to serve

Place the steak strips in the slow cooker dish and top with the chilli, ginger, garlic, cloves (if using) and stock. Make sure that the meat is completely immersed in the stock. Cover with the lid and cook on low for 8–10 hours or until the meat is wonderfully tender.

When you're ready to eat, place the noodles in a large bowl and cover with boiling water. Leave to stand for 4 minutes. Drain thoroughly, then divide among 4 deep serving bowls. Top each one with a handful of bean sprouts, some spring onion, chopped coriander and mint.

Season the hot stock with the lime juice and fish sauce to taste. Top the noodles with the cooked beef and then ladle over the hot stock. Garnish with a few whole mint and coriander leaves. Serve immediately with lime wedges to squeeze over.

Chinese red braised beef

PREPARATION TIME: 10 MINUTES
COOKING TIME: 8–12 HOURS
SERVES 4–6

Brisket needs long, moist cooking to bring out its gloriously rich and almost sweet flavour. Cooking it in flavoured stock or sauce helps even more – which is why this recipe is so good!

1.5kg (3¼lb) brisket joint
2 garlic cloves, peeled and left whole
150ml (5fl oz) light soy sauce
100ml (3½fl oz) dry sherry

1 tsp toasted sesame oil
1 tsp shredded fresh root ginger
½ tbsp Chinese five-spice powder
Pared rind of 1 orange
150ml (5fl oz) cold water

Place all of the ingredients in the slow cooker dish and mix well.

Cover with the lid and cook on low for 8 hours, or for up to 12 hours, until the meat is meltingly tender.

Remove the meat from the slow cooker dish and carve into thick slices. Drizzle with the sauce and serve with noodles and steamed green vegetables.

TRY...
this recipe with a lighter vegetable stock in the summer months, or flavour it with summer herbs and white wine for a more European option.

Spaghetti and meatballs

PREPARATION TIME: 15 MINUTES

COOKING TIME: 8 HOURS

SERVES 4

A family classic made extra flavoursome and rich with long, slow cooking. This is great with a green salad.

1 large onion, peeled and finely diced

1 green pepper, deseeded and finely diced

1 garlic clove, peeled and crushed

2 x 400g (14oz) tins chopped tomatoes

2 tbsp tomato purée

1 tbsp soft dark brown sugar

1 tsp dried oregano

2 bay leaves

Sea salt and freshly ground black pepper

For the meatballs:

500g (1lb 2oz) lean beef mince

1 egg, slightly beaten

2 tbsp finely grated Parmesan cheese, plus extra to serve

½ tsp sea salt

Place the onion and diced pepper in the slow cooker dish together with the remaining sauce ingredients. Mix well and season with salt and pepper. Cover with the lid and cook on high while you prepare the meatballs.

Place the mince into a large mixing bowl and add the egg, Parmesan cheese and salt. Mix well with your hand for at least 2–3 minutes or until the mince is smooth and blended very thoroughly with the other ingredients.

Dampen your clean hands with cold water and roll the mince mixture into 16 even, walnut-sized balls. When they are all prepared drop them gently into the slow cooker dish. Using a wooden spoon or spatula, carefully fold the meatballs into the sauce, being careful not to break them up. Cover with the lid and reduce the temperature to low. Cook for 8 hours, without stirring, until the sauce has thickened and the meatballs are tender.

Stir gently to mix and season to taste. Discard the bay leaves and serve spooned over hot, freshly cooked spaghetti with plenty of grated Parmesan.

Lamb massaman curry

PREPARATION TIME: 10 MINUTES
COOKING TIME: 8–9 HOURS
SERVES 4

This rich, creamy curry is wonderfully aromatic and spicy. Massaman paste is available at most major supermarkets.

1 x 400ml (14fl oz) tin coconut milk
5–6 tsp massaman curry paste
600g (1lb 5oz) lamb shoulder, cut into chunks
1 onion, peeled, halved and finely sliced
1 aubergine, cut into chunks

1 red pepper, deseeded and cut into chunks
250g (9oz) baby new potatoes, washed and halved
2–3 tbsp fish sauce, to taste
Fresh coriander leaves, to garnish
Lime wedges, to serve

Pour the coconut milk into the slow cooker dish and mix in the massaman paste. Add the lamb and the vegetables and mix well.

Cover with the lid and cook on low for 8–9 hours or until the lamb is tender and the sauce has thickened slightly.

Add the fish sauce to taste, then garnish with coriander leaves and serve with lime wedges for squeezing over accompanied with freshly cooked rice or noodles.

WHAT ABOUT...

making a vegetarian version using sweet potato or squash in place of the lamb. Check the curry paste you're using though as some brands have shrimp paste as an ingredient and are not suitable for vegetarians.

Easy spaghetti bolognese

PREPARATION TIME: 10 MINUTES
COOKING TIME: 6–8 HOURS
SERVES 8

Beef mince should almost always be full fat – the fat giving it a wonderful flavour and texture. However, there are times when extra lean mince is perfect, and this recipe is one of them. Use good-quality extra lean beef mince with about 5% fat, add lots of vegetables and it's as easy as that.

1 large onion, peeled and diced

2 large carrots, peeled and diced

2 celery sticks, trimmed and cut
  into 1cm (½in) pieces

3 garlic cloves, peeled and roughly
  chopped

550g (1lb 4oz) extra lean, 5% fat
  beef mince

2 beef stock cubes

250ml (9fl oz) red wine

2 tbsp concentrated tomato purée

1 tsp good-quality dried oregano

4 x 400g (14oz) tins chopped
  tomatoes

Sea salt and freshly ground black
  pepper

About 2 tbsp caster sugar, or
  to taste

Freshly grated Parmesan cheese,
  for sprinkling

Place the vegetables and garlic into the slow cooker dish. Crumble the mince and the stock cube over the vegetables, add the red wine, tomato purée, oregano and tomatoes and mix well, using the spoon to break up any large lumps of mince.

Cover with the lid and cook on high for 6–8 hours, stirring occasionally if you are around, until reduced and the tomato has cooked down. Season generously with salt and pepper, and the sugar to taste.

Serve on a bed of freshly cooked spaghetti with plenty of Parmesan cheese sprinkled over, and a green salad on the side.

TRY...
adding some dried chilli flakes at the beginning and a tin of drained red kidney beans 30 minutes before the end of cooking for an easy chilli to serve with rice.

Spiced lamb pilaf

PREPARATION TIME: 15 MINUTES
COOKING TIME: 8 ½–9 ½ HOURS
SERVES 4

This Moroccan-inspired pilaf is fantastic – fragrant and spicy with plenty of different textures and tons of flavour. Most importantly, the slow cooking leaves the lamb neck irresistibly tender.

½ tbsp olive oil
500g (1lb 2oz) lamb neck fillet, cut into 3cm (1¼in) pieces
2 red onions, peeled and finely sliced
½ tsp dried red chilli flakes
2 garlic cloves, peeled and crushed
50g (2oz) pine nuts

1 tsp ground coriander
½ tsp turmeric
1 tsp ground ginger
1 tsp ground cinnamon
400ml (14fl oz) white wine
Sea salt and freshly ground black pepper
200g (7oz) basmati rice

Warm half of the oil in a frying pan over a high heat. When hot, add the lamb and cook until browned on all sides. Spoon into the slow cooker dish.

Return the pan to the heat and add the remaining oil. Reduce the heat to medium and add the onions, chilli, garlic, pine nuts, coriander, turmeric, ginger and cinnamon and cook for about 5 minutes or until the spices are wonderfully aromatic and the onion is softened. Reduce the heat during cooking if the spices or pine nuts start to burn.

Add the wine to the pan and mix well. Bring to the boil, then pour this over the lamb. Season generously with salt and pepper. Cover with the lid and cook on low for 8–9 hours.

When you get back from work or 30 minutes before you want to eat, place the rice in a sieve. Pour a kettle full of freshly boiled water over the rice and drain. Fold the wet rice into the lamb mixture.

Cover with the lid again and cook for a further 30 minutes or until the rice is tender and has absorbed most of the cooking liquid. Season to taste.

Irish stew

PREPARATION TIME: 10 MINUTES

COOKING TIME: 9 HOURS

SERVES 6–8

Far from the greasy, fatty Irish stew of school dinners of old, this fresh-tasting version is fantastic, and as good in the summer as it is in the depths of winter.

1 large onion, peeled and finely sliced

2 large carrots, peeled and roughly chopped

3 celery sticks, trimmed and roughly chopped

850g (1lb 14oz) lamb neck fillet, cut into 3cm (1¼in) chunks

6 tbsp pearl barley

450g (1lb) potatoes, such as Maris Piper, peeled and diced into 3cm (1¼in) chunks

2 x 400g (14oz) tins chopped tomatoes

Sea salt and freshly ground black pepper

Roughly chopped fresh mint and flat leaf parsley, to serve

Mix the onion, carrots and celery together in a bowl. Using about a third of the vegetables, make a layer over the base of the slow cooker dish. Top with about a third of the lamb, then one of pearl barley and potatoes, and finally a layer of tomatoes. Season generously with salt and pepper and repeat again, twice, to make three layers, finishing with tomatoes.

Cover with the lid and cook on low for 9 hours or until the sauce has thickened and the lamb and potatoes are wonderfully tender. Sprinkle with the chopped mint and parsley before serving.

WHAT ABOUT...

if you want to use the oven? Place in a casserole dish with a tight-fitting lid in an oven preheated to 180°C (350°F), Gas mark 4 for 2–3 hours or until the lamb is tender.

Tomato-simmered lamb shanks

PREPARATION TIME: 5 MINUTES
COOKING TIME: 8–9 HOURS
SERVES 4

The rich, sweet meat on lamb shanks works wonderfully with the sweetness and slight acidity of the tomato sauce in this recipe. If shanks aren't available try using lamb shoulder instead.

1 red onion, peeled, halved and finely sliced

2 garlic cloves, peeled and finely sliced

1 large fresh rosemary sprig

2 x 400g (14oz) tins chopped tomatoes

100ml (3½fl oz) red wine

Sea salt and freshly ground black pepper

4 lamb shanks, about 350g (12oz) each

Mix the onion, garlic, rosemary, tomatoes and wine together in the slow cooker dish. Season well with salt and pepper.

Fit the shanks in a snug single layer on top and push them down into the tomato mixture so that they are immersed in the sauce.

Cover with the lid and cook on low for 8–9 hours. The meat will have produced lots of fat during cooking, so spoon off as much of this from the surface of the stew as possible and discard. Serve the shanks with couscous or mash and a large green salad.

WHAT ABOUT...

if you want to use the oven? Place in a casserole dish, cover with a tight-fitting lid or foil and cook in an oven preheated to 170°C (325°F), Gas mark 3 for 4–6 hours.

Liver and bacon

PREPARATION TIME: 15 MINUTES
COOKING TIME: 6–8 HOURS
SERVES 4

A school lunch classic that seems to be as polarising now as it ever was! However, this simple casserole is well worth trying even if you're not a liver fan; if you are, you'll love it.

1 tbsp olive oil

4 rashers smoked streaky bacon, diced

2 onions, peeled and finely sliced

500g (1lb 2oz) lamb's liver portions

2 tbsp plain flour

Sea salt and freshly ground black pepper

500ml (18fl oz) red wine

2 fresh thyme sprigs

2 bay leaves

Warm the olive oil in a large frying pan over a medium heat. When hot, add the bacon and fry briefly before adding the onions. Cook for about 5 minutes or until golden and softened slightly. Spoon into the slow cooker dish.

Return the pan to the heat. Place the liver, flour and seasoning into a freezer bag, seal and toss quickly to coat. Add the liver to the hot pan and sear for about 1 minute on each side or until browned. Add to the slow cooker dish.

Pour in the wine and add the herbs. Cover with the lid and cook on low for 6–8 hours or until the liver is tender and the sauce is thickened. Serve with buttered jacket potatoes and seasonal vegetables.

WHAT ABOUT...

if you want to use the oven? Follow the recipe through steps 1 and 2, then place in a casserole dish, cover with a tight-fitting lid or foil and cook in an oven preheated to 170°C (375°F), Gas mark 3 for 1–2 hours.

Easy pork cassoulet

PREPARATION TIME: 5 MINUTES
COOKING TIME: 6–8 HOURS
SERVES 4

Cassoulet is such a rich and rewarding dish and it really benefits from slow cooking. This easy version does cut some corners but still produces a fantastic result for those with less time for preparation – it's also really economical to make.

500g (1lb 2oz) diced pork shoulder
1 onion, peeled and diced
2 rashers streaky bacon, diced
2 tbsp tomato purée
2 garlic cloves, peeled and finely sliced
1 x 400g (14oz) tin chopped tomatoes

1 x 410g tin cannellini beans, drained and rinsed
1 tbsp caster sugar, to taste
Sea salt and freshly ground black pepper
1 tbsp chopped fresh flat leaf parsley

Throw everything other than the parsley into the slow cooker dish and mix well.

Cover with the lid and cook on low for 6 hours or for up to 8 hours.

Season to taste with salt and pepper. Spoon into shallow bowls and sprinkle with the chopped parsley. Serve with plenty of crusty bread and a green salad.

TRY...
making a double batch and freezing in portions – perfect ready meals for those days when you don't feel like cooking.

Slow-cooked sausages in cider

PREPARATION TIME: 10 MINUTES
COOKING TIME: 6–8 HOURS
SERVES 4

Sausages are quick to cook but here they really benefit from long, slow cooking in a tasty apple sauce. If you're making this for children use apple juice instead of the cider.

2 tsp olive oil
8 good-quality, thick pork
  sausages
150g (5oz) rashers smoked streaky
  bacon, cut into cubes
2 trimmed leeks, cleaned and cut
  into 2cm (¾in) slices

3 eating apples, peeled, cored and
  diced
300ml (10fl oz) cider or apple juice
Flat-leaf parsley leaves, to garnish

Warm the olive oil in a large frying pan over a medium heat. When hot, add the sausages and cook for 5 minutes or until evenly browned. Remove from the pan and spoon into the slow cooker dish.

Return the frying pan to the heat, add the bacon and leeks and stir-fry over a medium heat for 3–5 minutes until just beginning to soften and colour. Spoon into the slow cooker dish.

Add the apples to the slow cooker together with the cider or apple juice. Cover with the lid and cook on low for 6–8 hours.

Spoon the sausages onto warm serving plates and scatter the parsley over the top. Serve with lashings of creamy mash and freshly steamed purple sprouting broccoli.

TRY...
This dish reheats really well either from chilled or frozen so it's perfect for making ahead.

Pork with braised red cabbage and apple

PREPARATION TIME: 10 MINUTES
COOKING TIME: 6–8 HOURS
SERVES 6

This warming winter dish is actually really good in the summer months too and is great served with steamed green beans or broccoli.

25g (1oz) butter

1 large onion, peeled and finely sliced

½ tsp ground allspice

¼ tsp freshly grated nutmeg

1 small red cabbage, cored and finely sliced

1 Bramley apple, peeled, cored and diced

4 tbsp red wine vinegar

2 tbsp light muscovado sugar

100ml (3½fl oz) cold water

Sea salt and freshly ground black pepper

1–1.5kg (2¼lb–3lb 5oz) pork shoulder

2 tbsp redcurrant jelly

Melt the butter in a pan over a medium heat, add the onion and cook for 5 minutes or until softened but not browned. Spoon into the slow cooker dish.

Stir the spices into the slow cooker dish, then add the cabbage, apple, red wine vinegar, sugar and cold water. Stir until thoroughly mixed and the sugar has dissolved. Season generously with salt and pepper. Top with the pork and push down – the cooker will be really full at this point and may need some coaxing to get the lid on! Cover with the lid and cook on low for 6–8 hours.

Remove the meat and leave it to rest. Alternatively, if you like crackling, preheat the grill to its highest setting and cook skin side up for about 3 minutes or until crisp and puffed-up. Stir the redcurrant jelly into the cabbage and season to taste.

Carve the meat into thick slices and serve on a bed of cabbage with any cooking juices drizzled over.

Traditional-style pork vindaloo

PREPARATION TIME: 15 MINUTES
COOKING TIME: 8–9 HOURS
SERVES 4

You'll be pleased you made your own, but if you really don't have time to make the spice paste, use 3–4 tablespoons of ready-made vindaloo paste, available from most supermarkets.

2 medium onions, peeled and finely sliced
500g (1lb 2oz) pork fillet, whole
250ml (9fl oz) hot vegetable stock

For the spice paste:
½–1 tsp dried chilli flakes, to taste
1 tsp cumin seeds
½ tsp black peppercorns
½ tsp cardamom seeds, about 15 pods
½ tsp ground cinnamon

½ tsp whole black mustard seeds
½ tsp fenugreek seeds
½ tbsp ground coriander
½ tsp turmeric
200ml (7fl oz) port
½ tsp sea salt
2 tsp dark brown muscovado sugar
2 garlic cloves, peeled and crushed
2.5cm (1in) cube fresh root ginger, peeled and finely diced

To make the spice paste, grind the chilli flakes, cumin seeds, peppercorns, cardamom seeds, cinnamon, black mustard seeds, fenugreek seeds, coriander and turmeric in a food processor or in a mortar with a pestle until a fine powder forms.

Transfer the ground spices to a small bowl and add the port, salt, sugar, garlic and ginger. Mix well and set aside.

Arrange the onions in a single layer in the slow cooker dish. Place the pork on top and pour over the spice mix and stock.

Cover with the lid and cook on low for 8–9 hours or until the pork is tender. Remove the pork from the slow cooker dish with tongs and place on a board or plate. Using two forks, shred the meat into large pieces. Return the pork to the slow cooker dish and mix well to coat in the sauce. Serve with freshly cooked basmati rice and a cucumber and mint raita.

GET-TOGETHERS

Cooking for family and friends
is easy, as the slow cooker does
all the hard work for you.

A meal in 6–9 hours.

Classic bouillabaisse

PREPARATION TIME: 15 MINUTES
COOKING TIME: 4½–5½ HOURS, PLUS PREHEATING
SERVES 6

This glorious blend of flavours is simple to make despite the relatively long list of ingredients. Ask your fishmonger for any decent offcuts and use these in place of prime fillets, if you prefer. Rouille is available fresh or in jars from most supermarkets, good fishmongers or delicatessens.

700g (1lb 9oz) raw tiger prawns
1 tbsp olive oil
1 garlic clove, peeled and crushed
1 trimmed leek, cleaned and
  roughly chopped
1 fennel bulb, trimmed and
  roughly chopped
1 dried red chilli
1 bay leaf, broken
A large pinch of saffron strands
Pared rind of ½ orange
1 x 400g (14oz) tin chopped
  tomatoes

250ml (9fl oz) dry white wine
1.3 litres (2¼ pints) boiling water
Sea salt and freshly ground black
  pepper
750g (1lb 10oz) firm white fish
  fillets, cut into large chunks
500g (1lb 2oz) live mussels,
  cleaned and beards removed (see
  page 96)
6 tbsp roughly chopped fresh flat
  leaf parsley

Preheat the slow cooker on high for 30 minutes. Remove the shells from the prawns and set aside. De-vein the prawns if necessary, then put them in a large bowl, cover and leave in the fridge until needed.

Add the olive oil to the hot slow cooker dish followed by the reserved prawn shells, the garlic, leek, fennel, chilli, bay leaf, saffron and orange rind and mix well to combine. Cover with the lid and cook for 1 hour or until the shells are pink and the mixture is wonderfully fragrant.

Uncover and add all but about 2 tablespoons of the tomatoes, the wine and the boiling water. Cover with the lid and cook for a further 2–3 hours or until the vegetables have started to break down.

Ladle the mixture in batches into a food processor (including the prawn shells) and blitz until smooth. Strain through a sieve, pushing as much of the solids through as possible with the back of a ladle. Season to taste with salt and pepper and set aside in a cool place until needed.

Return the now clean slow cooker dish to the base and preheat again on high for 30 minutes. Add the strained stock, then cover with the lid and cook for a further 30–60 minutes or until piping hot.

Carefully add the fish, mussels and reserved tomatoes and prawns. Cover and cook for another 30 minutes or until the mussels have just opened and the prawns are pink. Remove and discard any mussels that have not opened. Sprinkle with the parsley and serve immediately with plenty of crusty bread to mop up the juices, and spoonfuls of rouille (see below).

TRY...
making your own 'cheat's' rouille. Blitz a char-grilled, peeled and deseeded red pepper in a food processor with a deseeded, chopped red chilli, $1/2$ crushed garlic clove, 1 tablespoon of lemon juice and a few tablespoons of good-quality mayonnaise until thick. Season to taste and transfer to a serving bowl. If not using immediately, cover with cling film and store in the fridge. It should be eaten on the day it is made.

Mussels with cream and saffron

PREPARATION TIME: 15 MINUTES
COOKING TIME: 2½-3 HOURS
SERVES 2 AS A MAIN COURSE OR 4 AS A STARTER

This recipe is fabulous for entertaining. All the preparation is done in advance, leaving you to just tip the mussels into the slow cooker shortly before your guests arrive. By the time you have had some pre-dinner drinks supper is ready.

1kg (2¼lb) live mussels
25g (1oz) butter
1 celery stick, trimmed and finely diced
2 trimmed leeks, white part only, cleaned and finely diced
1 bay leaf
1 fresh thyme sprig

2 tsp curry powder
A pinch of cayenne pepper
A large pinch of saffron strands
250ml (9fl oz) white wine
300ml (10fl oz) fish stock
200ml (7fl oz) double cream
Sea salt and freshly ground black pepper

Wash the mussels under cold running water and remove the beards or hairy bits from each one. Discard any broken or open shells and any mussels that do not close when tapped sharply on the edge of the sink.

Place the butter, vegetables, herbs and spices, wine and stock in the slow cooker dish. Cover with the lid and cook on low for 2 hours or until the vegetables are very soft.

Increase the heat to high. Leave for 15–30 minutes to warm up, then add the cream and prepared mussels. Season with salt and pepper and mix well to coat all the shells in the cooking liquid. Cover again and cook for a further 15–30 minutes or until the mussels have opened.

Stir the mussels again so that the open shells fill with the creamy sauce (discard any unopened mussels). Spoon into warm bowls and serve with crusty bread to mop up the juices.

Wild mushroom open lasagne

PREPARATION TIME: 20 MINUTES
COOKING TIME: 4 HOURS
SERVES 4

A real treat when wild mushrooms are in season.

100g (3½oz) chilled butter, cubed, plus extra for greasing
750g (1lb 10oz) mixed wild mushrooms, such as morels, ceps and shiitake, wiped and cut into large wedges or thick slices
2 tbsp olive oil
Sea salt and freshly ground black pepper

3 tbsp dry white wine
1 garlic clove, peeled and crushed
16 sheets fresh or dried lasagne
200ml (7fl oz) crème fraiche
2 tbsp finely chopped fresh parsley
50g (2oz) freshly grated Parmesan cheese, plus extra to serve

Butter the inside of the slow cooker dish. Place the mushrooms in the dish, add half of the butter, olive oil, 1 teaspoon of salt, the wine and garlic and mix well. Cover with the lid and cook on low for 4 hours or until softened.

About 30 minutes before you wish to eat, bring a large saucepan of salted water to the boil over a high heat. Place a clean tea towel onto a clean surface. Drop each lasagne sheet into the water for 1 minute or according to the packet instructions, then remove with a slotted spoon and place onto the prepared tea towel. Repeat with the other sheets, placing them in a single layer on the tea towel and interleaving them with more tea towels as required so that the lasagne sheets do not touch each other.

Place the crème fraîche and remaining butter in a small saucepan and warm over a medium heat until the butter has melted, then whisk the mixture until combined. Season the mushrooms and add the parsley.

Preheat the grill to its highest setting. Place a sheet of lasagne onto a warm deep serving plate. Top with a spoonful of the mushroom mixture and a drizzle of the crème fraîche sauce. Repeat three times finishing with the sauce. Sprinkle with Parmesan cheese and cook under the grill for 2–3 minutes or until golden. Keep warm while you repeat with the other plates.

Mini chestnut, mushroom and red wine pies with mustard pastry

PREPARATION TIME: 35 MINUTES
COOKING TIME: 4 ½ HOURS
SERVES 6

VEGETARIAN

These tasty little pies are hearty and full of flavour – the fact that they're vegetarian is by the by!

1 tbsp olive oil

25g (1oz) butter, plus extra
for greasing

350g (12oz) mushrooms, sliced

Sea salt and freshly ground black
pepper

½ small onion, peeled and finely
sliced

2 garlic cloves, peeled and
crushed

1 tsp dried oregano

1 tbsp tomato purée

2 tbsp plain flour

200ml (7fl oz) red wine

150g (5oz) peeled cooked
chestnuts

For the pastry:

400g (14oz) self-raising flour, plus
extra for dusting

A large pinch of salt

200g (7oz) vegetable suet

4 tsp wholegrain mustard

About 200–300ml (7–10fl oz) cold
water

Warm half of the olive oil and the butter in a large frying pan over a high heat. When hot, add the mushrooms, then season with salt and pepper and cook for 5 minutes or until golden. Spoon into a large mixing bowl. Return the pan to the heat, add the onion and garlic and cook for a further 5 minutes until golden and softened, reducing the heat if they begin to catch on the base of the pan.

Stir in the oregano, tomato purée and flour to make a thick paste. Pour in the wine and mix well to combine. When the wine starts to boil continue stirring for another minute, then pour the mixture into the mixing bowl with the mushrooms. Roughly crumble the chestnuts into the mixture, season with salt and pepper and stir to coat all the ingredients in the sauce. Set aside to cool completely.

Butter 6 mini-pudding basins that will fit in a single layer in your slow cooker dish. Line the bases with small squares of parchment paper. Butter 6 x 15 x 15cm (6 x 6in) squares of foil and set aside.

For the pastry, sift the flour and salt into a large mixing bowl. Add the suet and mix well with your hands. Mix in the mustard and enough cold water to make a soft dough.

Take about one-quarter of the dough and turn out onto a lightly floured surface. Roll out the dough until it is about 5mm (^{1}/$_{4}$in) thick. Use one of the basins to cut out 6 rounds and set them aside for the pie lids.

Roll the remaining dough out until it is 5mm (^{1}/$_{4}$in) thick and cut into 6 large rounds, about 13–15cm (5–6in) across. Use these to line the prepared basins, pushing down into the base of each one. Leave about 1cm (^{1}/$_{2}$in) of pastry hanging over the top of the basins.

Spoon the cooled mushroom mixture into the lined basins. Place the reserved lids on top and fold the overhanging dough around the edges over. Press together to seal, then cover with the greased foil, making a pleat in the centre as you go. Tie around the top of the basins tightly with string to stop any water getting in.

Place into the slow cooker dish and carefully pour enough boiling water around the outside to come about one-third of the way up the sides of the basins. Cover with the lid and cook on high for about 4 hours or until risen and the filling is piping hot. Remove from the slow cooker dish and leave to stand for 5 minutes. Run a sharp knife around the edges to loosen and then invert the pies onto serving plates to serve.

Preserved lemon and pine nut quinoa with sun-dried tomato sauce

PREPARATION TIME: 10 MINUTES

COOKING TIME: 3 HOURS

SERVES 4

VEGETARIAN

Quinoa (pronounced keen-wah) is a grain from South America now widely available in supermarkets. It is not dissimilar in texture to couscous and has an appealing nutty flavour.

6 preserved lemons (see page 74)

1 large onion, peeled, halved and cut into 1cm (½in) wedges

1 red chilli, deseeded and finely chopped

1 tbsp olive oil

1 tsp golden caster sugar

Sea salt and freshly ground black pepper

200g (7oz) quinoa

500ml (18fl oz) hot vegetable stock

50g (2oz) pine nuts

8 tbsp fresh coriander leaves

4 tbsp sun-dried tomato paste

8 tbsp boiling water

Cut the preserved lemons into quarters, then remove and discard the flesh. Shred the lemon skins into strips. Place the onion, strips of lemon skin, the chilli, olive oil and sugar in the slow cooker dish and season to taste with salt and pepper. Cover with the lid and cook on high for 2 hours or until the onion is very soft.

Add the quinoa and hot stock and mix well to combine. Cover again and cook for a further hour.

Meanwhile, warm a frying pan over a medium heat. When hot, add the pine nuts and cook for 3–5 minutes, shaking the pan frequently, until they are an even golden colour. Remove from the heat and set aside.

When the quinoa is tender, with just a little bite to it (like cooked rice or couscous), stir in the coriander and the reserved pine nuts. In a separate bowl, mix the tomato paste with the boiling water to make a thin sauce. Serve the quinoa on warm plates with rocket leaves and the tomato sauce drizzled around the edge.

Sea bass with tamarind and ginger

PREPARATION TIME: 15 MINUTES

COOKING TIME: 3 HOURS 5 MINUTES

SERVES 4

Sea bass is a good foil for this feisty spice paste. Packed with flavour, the paste is vibrant and zingy. The slow-cooking process enables the fish to cook and marinate simultaneously, ensuring a great taste.

2 x 900g (2lb) whole sea bass scaled, gutted and cleaned

2 tbsp sesame oil

1 red chilli, deseeded and roughly chopped

1 lemongrass stalk, peeled and roughly chopped

1 tbsp roughly chopped fresh root ginger

2 garlic cloves, peeled and crushed

4 kaffir lime leaves, roughly chopped

2 tsp tamarind paste

A small handful (about 10g/¼oz) of fresh coriander

100ml (3½fl oz) cold water

Fish sauce, to taste

Lime wedges, to serve

Using a sharp knife, slash each side of the fish about three times. Oil the inside of the slow cooker dish with some of the sesame oil.

Warm the remaining oil in a small frying pan over a low heat. When hot, add the chilli, lemongrass, ginger, garlic and lime leaves and stir-fry for 1–2 minutes or until very fragrant.

Spoon the hot mixture into a mini food processor, add the tamarind paste and coriander and blitz to make a rough paste. Spread the paste evenly over the fish. Arrange the fish in a single layer in the slow cooker dish. Drizzle over any remaining spice paste and add the cold water.

Cover with the lid and cook on low for about 3 hours or until soft when tested with the tip of a knife. Drizzle with fish sauce to taste, then divide the fish among 4 serving plates and spoon over some of the spicy cooking liquid. Serve with lime wedges and freshly cooked rice or noodles.

Skate wings with warm citrus and tomato salad

PREPARATION TIME: 10 MINUTES

COOKING TIME: 2 HOURS

SERVES 2

This is a fantastically flavoursome dish. It works really well with other white fish too like plaice, John Dory, cod or haddock.

6 mixed tomatoes (use different colours, sizes and shapes), thickly sliced

1 red chilli, deseeded and chopped

½ red onion, peeled and very finely sliced

1 tsp red wine vinegar

Finely grated zest and juice of 1 lemon (preferably unwaxed)

Finely grated zest and juice of 1 orange

Sea salt and freshly ground black pepper

2 tbsp cold water

2 skate wings, about 400g (14oz) each

2 tbsp finely chopped fresh mint leaves

1 tbsp finely chopped fresh basil

Extra virgin olive oil, for drizzling

Place the tomatoes in the slow cooker dish, then sprinkle with the chilli, onion, vinegar, lemon and orange zests. Season with salt and pepper, add the cold water and mix well.

Arrange the fish on top of the tomatoes in a single layer if possible, but don't worry if not. Cover with the lid and cook on low for 2 hours or until the fish is tender when tested with the tip of a knife.

Drizzle the lemon and orange juice over the fish and carefully place onto warm serving plates. Sprinkle the herbs over the tomatoes and then spoon onto the plates with the fish. Drizzle with extra virgin olive oil and serve with new potatoes and watercress.

Herb-infused bream with caramelised onions

PREPARATION TIME: 10 MINUTES
COOKING TIME: 3–3½ HOURS
SERVES 4

Red bream are firm-textured, well-flavoured fish that can take stronger flavourings like onions, garlic and anchovies. Choose small fish so you can serve one per person.

4 x 400–500g (14oz–1lb 2oz) red bream, cleaned, scaled and gutted

4 fresh thyme sprigs

4 fresh flat leaf parsley sprigs

Sea salt and freshly ground black pepper

600g (1lb 5oz) small red onions, peeled and thinly sliced

50g (2oz) tin anchovies in olive oil

2 garlic cloves, peeled and crushed

Finely grated zest and juice of 1 lemon (preferably unwaxed)

2 tsp caster sugar

Score the bream three times on each side and remove the side fins with scissors. Pack the thyme and parsley into the cavities and season all over with salt and pepper.

Place the onions in the slow cooker dish. Drain the anchovies, reserving the oil, and chop as finely as possible. Mix with the garlic, anchovy oil and lemon zest and juice, then season with pepper and add the sugar. Mix into the onion mixture.

Cover with the lid and cook on high for 2 hours, stirring occasionally, until the onions are beginning to caramelise.

Arrange the fish in a single layer on top of the onions, then cover and cook for a further 1–1½ hours or until the fish is cooked through and opaque. Serve each fish on a bed of onions, with new potatoes and green vegetables.

Coq au vin blanc

PREPARATION TIME: 15 MINUTES
COOKING TIME: 8–9 HOURS
SERVES 6

Try this lighter version of the French classic using white wine instead of the more usual red.

12 chicken thighs

50g (2oz) rashers streaky bacon, diced

50g (2oz) plain flour

1 large onion, peeled, halved and finely sliced

2 garlic cloves, peeled and finely sliced

500g (1lb 2oz) button mushrooms

500ml (18fl oz) dry white wine

Sea salt and freshly ground black pepper

Warm a large frying pan over a high heat. When hot, add the chicken thighs and bacon and cook for 5–10 minutes until golden on all sides. Spoon into the slow cooker dish. Sprinkle the flour over the meat and mix well to coat.

Return the frying pan to the heat, add the onion and garlic, reduce the heat to medium and cook for 5 minutes until the onion is softened but not coloured. Add to the chicken in the slow cooker dish.

Return the frying pan to a high heat once again and add the mushrooms – you may need to do this in a couple of batches if the pan isn't large enough. Fry for about 5 minutes for each batch or until the mushrooms are just beginning to colour. Add the wine and allow to bubble fiercely for 1–2 minutes before pouring over the chicken. Season well with salt and pepper. Cover with the lid and cook on low for 8–9 hours or until the chicken is tender and the sauce has thickened. Remove from the heat and serve with crusty bread and a green salad.

WHAT ABOUT...

if you want to use the oven? Cook in a casserole dish with a tight-fitting lid in an oven preheated to 150°C (300°F), Gas mark 2 for 4–6 hours.

Poussin with fig and ginger stuffing

PREPARATION TIME: 15 MINUTES

COOKING TIME: 3–4 HOURS

SERVES 2

These tender little birds work wonderfully with this sweet fig stuffing.

2 poussins, about 450–500g
 (1lb–1lb 2oz) each

Sea salt and freshly ground black
 pepper

25g (1oz) unsalted butter

3 just ripe figs, halved

2cm (¾in) piece fresh root ginger,
 peeled and grated

2 fresh thyme sprigs

4 rashers smoked streaky bacon

8 small shallots, peeled

400ml (14fl oz) ginger wine

Remove the string from the birds, rinse them under cold water and pat dry with kitchen paper. Season inside and out with salt and pepper. Cut half of the butter into 2 pieces. Place a piece of butter, 2 pieces of fig, ½ teaspoon of grated ginger and a sprig of thyme inside each cavity. Place the poussins in the slow cooker dish, smear the breasts with some more butter and lay 2 rashers of bacon over the top of each bird.

Melt the remaining butter in a sauté pan, add the shallots and fry over a medium-high heat for 5–10 minutes or until they become golden brown. Add the ginger wine and the remaining grated ginger and bring to the boil, then pour around the birds in the slow cooker dish. Cover with the lid and cook on low for 3–4 hours or until the juices run clear when a skewer is inserted into a leg. Remove the birds from the slow cooker and place them on an ovenproof serving plate.

Preheat the grill to its highest setting and grill the tops of the birds for 3–5 minutes or until the bacon is crispy. Keep the birds warm.

Warm a non-stick frying pan over a high heat. When hot, add the remaining fig halves cut side down and cook for 1–2 minutes or until just caramelised. Pour off some of the excess fat in the slow cooker dish, leaving just the meaty juices behind and pour these juices into the frying pan. Cook for a further 3–5 minutes or until it is reduced and slightly thickened. Season to taste, then pour the sauce around the birds.

Turkey 'saltimbocca' with vermouth butter sauce

PREPARATION TIME: 15 MINUTES
COOKING TIME: 1–1½ HOURS
SERVES 4

This twist on the Italian classic uses turkey instead of veal. It's perfect with the Parma ham and sage.

4 turkey breast steaks, about 500g (1lb 2oz) in total

4 large sage leaves

4 slices Parma ham

1 garlic clove, peeled

50ml (1¾fl oz) dry vermouth

50ml (1¾fl oz) cold water

25g (1oz) butter, cubed

Place the turkey steaks between two sheets of cling film and place on a large board. Using a meat mallet or the end of a rolling pin, bash out the steaks until they are no more than 1cm (½in) thick.

Top each flattened steak with a sage leaf followed by a slice of Parma ham, then with the ham on the outside, roll each steak up tightly, like a Swiss roll. Secure each one with a cocktail stick. Cut the garlic in half and rub the inside of the slow cooker dish with the cut edge. Add the vermouth and the cold water.

Place the turkey rolls in the slow cooker dish. Cover with the lid and cook on low for 2 hours or until the juices run clear when the tip of a sharp knife is inserted into the centre.

Remove from the slow cooker dish and leave to stand for 2 minutes. Meanwhile, strain the sauce through a sieve into a saucepan. Warm over a medium heat, then gradually whisk in the butter piece by piece until the sauce is glossy and slightly thickened.

Remove the cocktail sticks from the turkey and cut each one into 3 thick slices. Serve cut side up, with the sauce spooned over, accompanied by salad and new potatoes.

Whole duck with bitter orange sauce

PREPARATION TIME: 5 MINUTES
COOKING TIME: 3½–4 HOURS
SERVES 4–6

Cooking a whole duck in the oven can be a messy affair – the fat coating much of the inside of the oven and seemingly most of the kitchen too! Using the slow cooker is a much easier and cleaner option. Here, a whole duck is cooked simply but the resulting dish has a really sophisticated flavour.

2–2.5kg (4lb 8oz –5lb 8oz) free-
   range duck
2 large oranges, washed and dried
6 fresh thyme sprigs
4 tbsp coarse-cut marmalade

Remove the giblets and any excess fat from the inside of the bird and discard. Prick the skin all over with the tip of a sharp knife, then place the duck in a clean kitchen sink and pour a kettle of boiling water over the bird. This will help to remove some of the excess fat. Repeat this step again.

Place the duck in the slow cooker dish, cover with the lid and cook on low for 1 hour. After this time, carefully pour the fat away into a bowl (don't discard it as it will make the most fabulous roast potatoes). Cover again and continue cooking the duck for another hour, then pour off the fat again.

Cut one of the oranges in half and push this together with the herbs inside the cavity of the duck. Cut the remaining orange into slices and surround the duck with the orange slices. Spoon the marmalade over the top of the duck and use the back of the spoon to 'paint' any bits of the bird that you can see with the marmalade.

Increase the temperature to high, then cover with the lid and cook for a further 2 hours or if you prefer your duck rare cook for 1–1½ hours.

Carefully lift the bird out of the slow cooker dish onto a board, draining off any juices that may have gathered in the cavity. Cover with a tent of foil and leave to rest in a warm place for about 15 minutes.

Pour off the excess fat in the slow cooker dish, leaving only the meaty cooking juices behind. If the juices have begun to cool, pour them into a small saucepan and warm over a medium heat for 2–3 minutes. Carve the duck and serve with the orange slices and the hot sauce spooned over.

TRY...
You can use duck legs with the skin on, if you prefer, and cook on low for 1 hour to remove the excess fat, then on high for 1 hour with orange slices, marmalade and herbs as above.

Turkey with apple and pecan butter

PREPARATION TIME: 20 MINUTES

COOKING TIME: 4–6 HOURS

SERVES 8–10

A turkey isn't just for Christmas – this recipe is perfect for summer celebrations and family gatherings.

2–3kg (2¼lb–6½lb) free-range
  turkey crown
1 red eating apple, cored
1 tbsp lemon juice
200g (7oz) unsalted butter,
  softened

50g (2oz) pecan nuts, finely
  chopped
2 tbsp chopped fresh tarragon
100ml (3½fl oz) dry white wine
Sea salt and freshly ground black
  pepper

Place the turkey on a large board and push your hand between the skin and the breast either side of the breastbone, to make 2 pockets. Cut 2 horizontal slices from the apple and set aside. Coarsely grate the remaining apple, place in a bowl with the lemon juice and mix well until the apple is coated in the juice. Place the butter in a large mixing bowl and mash with a fork to soften. Add the pecans, tarragon and grated apple and mix well.

Using your hand, push the flavoured butter into the 2 pockets in the turkey. Divide it evenly between either side, being sure to push the butter all the way along each breast. Finish by sliding the reserved apple slices on top of the butter, one either side of the breastbone.

Place the crown in the slow cooker dish and cook on low for 4–6 hours or until the juices run clear when the thickest part of the meat is pierced with a skewer. Lift the crown out of the dish, cover with a tent of foil and leave in a warm place to rest for at least 30 minutes, or for up to 60 minutes.

Meanwhile, carefully pour or spoon off the fat in the slow cooker dish, leaving the meaty juices behind. Pour these juices into a saucepan and bring to the boil over a high heat. Add the wine and continue to boil for another 5 minutes or until reduced by at least half. Season to taste. Serve the turkey drizzled with the buttery sauce, new potatoes and vegetables.

Rabbit with apple and prune sauce

PREPARATION TIME: 5 MINUTES
COOKING TIME: 4 HOURS 10 MINUTES
SERVES 4

This full-flavoured dish tastes like it has been prepared in a restaurant – only you will know how easy it is to make!

3 tbsp plain flour

Sea salt and freshly ground black
  pepper

4 rabbit legs

1 tbsp olive oil

25g (1oz) butter

1 onion, peeled and finely sliced

2 Bramley apples peeled, cored
  and diced

200ml (7fl oz) brandy

150g (5oz) dried ready-to-eat
  prunes

Place the flour in a large freezer bag and season with salt and pepper. Add the rabbit legs and toss to coat evenly. Shake the legs to remove any excess flour, but keep any leftover flour in the bag.

Warm the olive oil and butter in a large frying pan over a medium heat. When hot, add the rabbit legs and cook for 5–10 minutes or until golden brown all over. Place the rabbit legs in the slow cooker dish.

Return the frying pan to the heat, add the onion and apples plus any extra flour and mix well. Add the brandy and cook for about 1 minute. Pour over the rabbit and scatter the prunes over the top.

Cover with the lid and cook on high for 4 hours or until tender. Serve with steamed green vegetables and new potatoes.

WHAT ABOUT...

if you want to use the oven? Place in a casserole dish, cover with a tight-fitting lid or foil and cook in an oven preheated to 150°C (300°F), Gas mark 2 for 3–4 hours or until tender. Check twice during cooking and add a little hot water if the mixture is drying out.

Pheasant with cider-brandy cream

PREPARATION TIME: 5 MINUTES
COOKING TIME: 6½ HOURS
SERVES 4

Pheasant is relatively low in fat and can dry out quickly so a slow cooker's moist heat is perfect for retaining its succulence.

350g (12oz) pheasant thigh fillets (about 8)
25g (1oz) plain flour
Sea salt and freshly ground black pepper
1 tbsp olive oil
1 onion, peeled, halved and finely sliced

1 Bramley apple, peeled, cored and diced
100ml (3½fl oz) cider brandy, such as Calvados or dry cider
100ml (3½fl oz) boiling water
2 bay leaves, halved
2 tbsp double cream

Place the pheasant in a large freezer bag with the flour. Season generously with salt and pepper before sealing the bag and tossing everything together until the meat is completely coated. Warm the olive oil in a large frying pan over a high heat. Add the pheasant and cook for 2 minutes on each side until just golden. Remove from the pan and place in the slow cooker dish.

Return the frying pan to the heat, add the onion and cook for 5 minutes, stirring frequently and reducing the heat if necessary, until golden brown. Mix in any remaining flour from the freezer bag and add the apple. Cook for a further minute or until thickened.

Stir the cider brandy into the onion mixture, scraping up any bits from the base of the pan as you do so. Allow to bubble for 30–60 seconds or until the brandy has reduced almost completely. Mix in the boiling water to loosen the mixture, then spoon the contents of the pan into the slow cooker dish. Add the bay leaves.

Cover with the lid and cook on low for 6 hours or until the pheasant is tender and the sauce is thick. Pour in the cream and fold into the sauce, adding a splash of boiling water if the sauce is too thick. Season to taste and serve with mounds of creamy mash.

Duck confit with sugared pistachio, orange and pomegranate salad

PREPARATION TIME: 10 MINUTES, PLUS CHILLING
COOKING TIME: 2
SERVES 4

This dish looks great, tastes great, and is great!

4 free-range duck legs
Sea salt and freshly ground black
  pepper
4 fresh thyme sprigs
50g (2oz) pistachios
1 tbsp golden caster sugar

200g (7oz) mixed baby salad
  leaves
2 spring onions, trimmed and
  finely shredded
1 pomegranate, halved
1 orange, cut into segments
Extra virgin olive oil, for drizzling

Rub the duck legs with 4 tablespoons of salt. Cover and place in the fridge for at least 1 hour. Dry the legs with kitchen paper, removing excess salt.

Place the thyme in the slow cooker dish and rest the duck legs on top. Cover with the lid and cook on low for 2 hours or until the duck is bathing in a pool of its own fat. Put the duck into a shallow dish together with the herbs and pour the liquid fat over the top to cover the duck completely. Leave to cool, then cover and chill until needed. It will keep for 2–3 days.

Thirty minutes before eating, remove the duck from the fridge. Put the pistachios and sugar in a small heavy-based saucepan and place over a high heat for 1–2 minutes until the sugar has just melted. Remove from the heat and stir to roughly coat the nuts in the caramel. Allow to cool, then roughly chop. Place the salad and onions on a large platter. Using a fork, release the seeds from the pomegranate, discarding any of the bitter white membrane. Scatter the seeds and orange segments over the salad.

Remove the duck from the now solidified fat and scrape off all the fat and skin. Using 2 forks, shred the flesh into bite-sized pieces and scatter the meat over the salad. Drizzle with a little olive oil, add seasoning to taste and scatter with the sugared pistachios. Serve straight away.

Wild Mushroom Open Lasagne

Mini Chestnut, Mushroom and Red Wine Pies with Mustard Pastry *(above)*
Duck Confit with Sugared Pistachio, Orange and Pomegranate Salad *(right)*

Italian Oxtail Stew *(above)* ● **Blueberry and Lime Loaf Cake** *(right)*

Blackberry and Apple Roly Poly *(left)* ● **Plum and Ginger Puddings** *(right)*

Fig Chutney

Slow-cooked venison with juniper, orange and whisky sauce

PREPARATION TIME: 10 MINUTES
COOKING TIME: 8–9 HOURS
SERVES 4

This rich dish is everything a venison casserole should be – warming, hearty and refined.

1 tbsp olive oil

400g (14oz) diced venison steak

8 shallots, peeled

250g (9oz) button mushrooms, wiped

25g (1oz) butter

1 heaped tsp juniper berries, lightly crushed

100ml (3½fl oz) whisky

2 tbsp plain flour

300ml (10fl oz) beef stock

1 fresh rosemary sprig

Juice of 1 orange

Sea salt and freshly ground black pepper

Warm the oil in a large frying pan over a medium heat, add the venison and cook for 5 minutes or until browned. Spoon the meat into the slow cooker dish.

Return the frying pan to the heat, add the shallots and mushrooms and cook for 5–10 minutes or until browned. Add the butter, juniper berries and whisky and allow to bubble for 1 minute.

Mix in the flour and half of the stock until smooth. Spoon into the slow cooker dish and add the remaining stock, the rosemary and orange juice.

Cover with the lid and cook on low for 8–9 hours or until the meat is wonderfully tender. Season to taste with salt and pepper and serve with dollops of creamy mash and steamed seasonal vegetables.

WHAT ABOUT...

if you want to use the oven? Simply place in a casserole dish, cover with a tight-fitting lid or foil and cook in an oven preheated to 150°C (300°F), Gas mark 2 for 4 hours or until the meat is wonderfully tender.

Lamb kleftico

PREPARATION TIME: 10 MINUTES
COOKING TIME: 6–8 HOURS
SERVES 6

Kleftico is a Greek dish with as many variations as you can imagine. Either way, to all intents and purposes it's a slow-cooked lamb dish with lemons, so here's another tasty version to add to the list.

1 tbsp olive oil
2.5kg (5lb 8oz) leg of lamb
 (bone in)
2 large onions, peeled and thinly
 sliced
1 tbsp dried oregano
2 garlic cloves, peeled and
 crushed

Sea salt and freshly ground black
 pepper
100ml (3½fl oz) white wine
600g (1lb 5oz) new potatoes
1 lemon, sliced

Warm the olive oil in a frying pan over a high heat. When hot, add the lamb and cook until browned on all sides.

Place the onions in the slow cooker dish and top with the seared lamb. Rub the top of the lamb with the oregano and garlic and season well with salt and pepper. Pour the white wine around the outside, then surround the meat with the new potatoes and add a layer of lemon slices on top of the potatoes.

Cover with the lid and cook on low for 6–8 hours or until the potatoes are tender and the meat is piping hot. Lift the meat out of the slow cooker dish and leave to rest under a tent of foil for about 10–15 minutes before carving (although the meat will be so tender you may find a spoon and a fork more useful for serving).

WHAT ABOUT...

if you want to use the oven? Cook in a large foil parcel in an oven preheated to 170°C (325°F), Gas mark 3 for 3–4 hours or until tender.

Rolled shoulder of lamb with cumin and harissa

PREPARATION TIME: 15 MINUTES
COOKING TIME: 4 HOURS
SERVES 4

This is so easy to make and so tasty. If you like your food spicy, then add more harissa. This dish is great served with wilted spinach.

800g (1lb 12oz) boneless lamb
  shoulder joint
1–2 tsp harissa paste, to taste
1 tsp cumin seeds
1 tbsp olive oil

500g (1lb 2oz) new potatoes,
  washed
150g (5oz) Greek yogurt
A large pinch of ground cumin

If the lamb is tied with string snip them with scissors and remove. Unroll the meat to give one flat piece, fat side down. Rub the harissa paste over the upper side of the meat and sprinkle with the cumin seeds. Roll the meat back up tightly and, using cooking string, tie the meat 3–4 times along the joint to stop it from springing open.

Warm the olive oil in a frying pan over a high heat. When hot, add the lamb and cook for about 5–10 minutes until the meat is browned all over.

Place the lamb in the slow cooker dish and pile the potatoes in around it. Cover with the lid and cook on low for 4 hours.

Spoon the yogurt into a serving dish and sprinkle with ground cumin. Serve the lamb in thick slices with the potatoes on the side and the fragrant yogurt to spoon over.

TRY...
using rolled pork shoulder or leg instead.

24-hour Persian lamb

PREPARATION TIME: 15 MINUTES
COOKING TIME: 24 HOURS
SERVES 6

Cooking lamb on the bone for such a long time makes it irresistibly tender and flavoursome. This recipe has to be tried!

1.5kg (3lb 5oz) lamb shoulder, bone in (depending on the size of your slow cooker – the meat should cover the base completely)

2 large pinches of saffron strands

1 large onion, peeled and roughly chopped

2 garlic cloves, peeled and roughly chopped

3cm (1¼in) piece fresh ginger root, peeled and roughly chopped

2 large pinches of dried chilli flakes

½ tsp turmeric

1 tsp garam masala

½ tbsp cumin seeds

6 tbsp Greek yogurt

1 tbsp chopped fresh mint leaves

Place the lamb in the slow cooker dish fat side up – the meat should cover the whole of the base of the slow cooker dish.

Soak the saffron in 2 tablespoons of warm water. Meanwhile, place all the remaining ingredients (except the yogurt and mint) in a food processor and blitz to make a rough paste. Add the saffron and its soaking water and blitz again to combine. Rub the paste over the upper surface of the lamb. Cover with the lid and cook on low for 24 hours. Carefully scrape the onion mixture from the surface of the lamb before lifting the meat out onto a board or serving platter.

Mix the yogurt into the onion mixture in the slow cooker dish, being sure to scrape up any caramelised bits on the base, then mix in the mint. Use a fork and spoon to 'carve' the meltingly tender lamb and serve topped with a spoonful of the sauce and accompanied by steamed green beans.

TRY...
this with a shoulder of pork. Make sure it has the bone in and that it will fit into your slow cooker.

Beef in Beaujolais

Brisket needs long, moist cooking to bring out its rich, sweet flavour.

1.5kg (3lb 5oz) brisket joint (rolled and tied)

2 celery sticks, trimmed and diced into 5mm (¼ in) cubes

2 carrots, peeled and diced into 5mm (¼ in) cubes

1 red onion, peeled and diced into 5mm (¼ in) cubes

4 garlic cloves, peeled and crushed

1 tbsp tomato purée

1 tbsp Dijon mustard

Sea salt and freshly ground black pepper

1 bottle Beaujolais or other light red wine

250ml (9fl oz) cold water

2 tbsp redcurrant jelly, or to taste

25g (1oz) butter, chilled and diced

Rinse the joint under cold running water and dry well with kitchen paper. Place the celery, carrot, and onion in the slow cooker dish.

Mix the garlic, tomato purée and mustard into the vegetables and season with salt and pepper. Pour in the wine and cold water and place the brisket on top of the vegetables. Cover with the lid and cook on low for 8–10 hours, basting with the red wine a couple of times. Remove the meat from the dish, cover in a tent of foil and leave to rest for 10 minutes. Meanwhile, strain the wine mixture through a sieve into a saucepan. Place the vegetables that are left behind in a bowl and keep warm.

Add the redcurrant jelly to the sauce in the pan. Bring to the boil over a high heat, then reduce the heat slightly and simmer vigorously for 10–15 minutes or until the sauce is reduced by at least half. Gradually whisk in the butter, piece by piece, until the sauce is glossy and slightly thickened.

Spoon the reserved vegetables into the centre of warm serving plates. Cut the beef into 6–8 thick slices and place a slice on top of the vegetables. Spoon the hot sauce over and serve immediately with buttered green vegetables and creamy mash.

Steak, ale and mushroom pudding

PREPARATION TIME: 15 MINUTES
COOKING TIME: 12–15 HOURS (SEE BELOW FOR A QUICKER OPTION)
SERVES 4–6

This traditional steamed pudding is full of mouth-watering slow-cooked beef in a rich ale sauce.

2 tbsp olive oil
1kg (2¼lb) diced braising steak
250g (9oz) chestnut mushrooms, wiped and sliced
1 onion, peeled and diced
1 carrot, peeled and diced
1 celery stick, trimmed and diced
3 fresh thyme sprigs
1 tbsp tomato purée
2 tbsp plain flour
300ml (10fl oz) ale or bitter
2 bay leaves, torn in half
A knob of butter, for greasing

For the pastry:
400g (14oz) self-raising flour, plus extra for dusting
A large pinch of salt
200g (7oz) shredded suet
2 tbsp finely chopped fresh flat leaf parsley
About 200–300ml (7–10fl oz) cold water

Warm the olive oil in a large pan over a high heat. When hot, add the beef in 3–4 batches and fry until well browned. Place into the slow cooker dish.

Return the pan to the heat, add the mushrooms and stir-fry for 3–5 minutes until golden. Add the diced vegetables, thyme, tomato purée and flour and mix well. Stir in the beer and bay leaves.

Pour the mixture into the slow cooker dish, scraping up any caramelised bits from the base of the pan as you go. Cover with the lid and cook on low overnight or for about 8–10 hours until the meat is very tender and the mixture has thickened slightly. Spoon into a bowl and leave to cool completely. Discard the bay leaves.

Butter a 1.7–2 litre (3–3½ pint) pudding basin that will fit in your slow cooker dish and line the base with a small square of parchment paper.

Take 2 large squares of foil about 50 x 50cm (20 x 20in) and sit one on top of the other. Butter the top sheet and set aside.

Sift the flour and salt into a large mixing bowl, add the suet and mix well with your hands, rubbing the suet in lightly. Gradually mix in the parsley and enough cold water to make a soft dough. Remove about one-quarter of the dough and set aside for the lid of the pie.

Turn the remainder out onto a lightly floured surface and roll out into a 40cm (16in) round about 5mm–1cm (^{1}/$_4$–^{1}/$_2$in) thick. Line the prepared basin with the dough, pushing it down into the base of the dish. Leave about 1cm (^{1}/$_2$in) of pastry hanging over the top of the basin.

Spoon the cooled beef mixture into the lined basin. Roll out the remaining dough into a round large enough to make a lid for the basin and place it on top of the beef mixture. Fold the overhanging dough around the edges over the top and press together to seal. Cover with the greased foil, making a pleat in the centre as you go. Tie around the top of the basin tightly with string to stop any water getting in.

Place the basin in the slow cooker dish and carefully pour enough boiling water around the outside to come about one-third of the way up the sides of the basin. Cover with the lid and cook on high for about 4–5 hours or until risen and the filling is piping hot. Remove from the slow cooker dish and leave to stand for 5 minutes. Run a sharp knife around the edge to loosen it and then invert onto a plate to serve.

WHAT ABOUT...
if you don't have time to slow-cook the meat mixture? Simply cover the pan at the end of step 3 and continue cooking on the hob for about 30 minutes. Leave to cool completely before continuing from step 4.

Beef in beer with horseradish dumplings

PREPARATION TIME: 10 MINUTES
COOKING TIME: 8 HOURS
SERVES 6–8

Comfort food at its best – but sophisticated with it! Use fresh horseradish if you can get it, but if not, most supermarkets sell jars of good-quality grated hot horseradish.

1.4kg (3lb) beef leg slices (bone removed)

2 celery sticks, trimmed and diced

2 carrots, peeled and diced

1 large onion, peeled and diced

1 tbsp tomato purée

1 tbsp plain flour

500ml (18fl oz) can ale or lager

3 bay leaves, torn in half

Sea salt and freshly ground black pepper

For the dumplings:

150g (5oz) shredded suet

150g (5oz) self-raising flour, plus extra for dusting

4 tsp grated horseradish

About 100ml (3½fl oz) cold water

Place the beef in the slow cooker dish and add the celery, carrots, onion, tomato purée and flour and mix well.

Pour the beer into the slow cooker dish, then add the bay leaves and season well with salt and pepper. Cover with the lid and cook on high for 6 hours or until rich and tender.

At this point start making the dumplings. Using your hands, mix the suet, flour and horseradish together in a large bowl. Season and add just enough cold water to bring the mixture together to a soft dough.

With very well-floured hands, divide the mixture into 6–8 portions and roll into balls, adding more flour to your hands as you need it. Place the dumplings around the edge of the slow cooker dish in a single layer.

Cover again and cook for a further 2 hours or until the dumplings are risen and soft. Serve immediately with plenty of seasonal green vegetables.

Italian oxtail stew

PREPARATION TIME: 5 MINUTES

COOKING TIME: 12–15 HOURS

SERVES 4–6

Rustic it may be. Simple, yes, but this gloriously rich stew is absolutely amazing. Perfect for the family and just as good for entertaining. Start with good-quality oxtail from a reputable butcher or supermarket and you won't go wrong.

1.5kg (3lb 5oz) oxtail pieces

1 tbsp olive oil

75g (3oz) pancetta, cubed

150ml (5fl oz) dry white wine

1 red onion, peeled and thinly sliced

4 garlic cloves, peeled and thinly sliced

4 whole cloves

2 x 400g (14oz) tins chopped tomatoes

Sea salt and freshly ground black pepper

1 lemon (preferably unwaxed)

Rinse the oxtail under cold running water and pat dry with kitchen paper. Warm the olive oil and pancetta in a large frying pan over a high heat. When hot, add the oxtail and cook for 10–15 minutes, turning occasionally, until all the pieces are browned.

Add the wine to the pan – be careful, it will bubble angrily at first. As soon as it calms down to a manageable level, pour into the slow cooker dish, then add the onion, garlic, cloves and tomatoes and mix well.

Cover with the lid and cook on low for 12–15 hours. Season to taste with salt and pepper. Using a very fine grater, zest the lemon over the oxtail, then serve immediately with green beans and plenty of creamy mash to soak up the juices.

WHAT ABOUT...

if you want to use the oven? Place everything in a casserole dish, cover with a tight-fitting lid or foil and cook in an oven preheated to 150°C (300°F), Gas mark 2 for 5–6 hours.

Slow-roasted pork belly with lentils and tarragon

PREPARATION TIME: 10 MINUTES
COOKING TIME: 6½ HOURS
SERVES 4–6

Tarragon is an ideal accompaniment to the pork and, rather than dominate, it gives the dish a wonderfully rounded flavour.

1–1.5kg (2lb 4oz–3lb 5oz) pork belly joint (the joint needs to fit into your slow cooker flat, without being folded or rolled)
Sea salt and freshly ground black pepper
4 celery sticks, trimmed and cut into diagonal slices
2 large red onions, peeled and cut into thin wedges
4 garlic cloves, peeled and left whole
3 fresh tarragon sprigs
200g (7oz) Puy lentils
½ bottle red wine

Unroll the pork belly if you need to so that you have a flat rectangular piece of meat and dry thoroughly with kitchen paper. If the skin on the belly has not been scored, then use a very sharp knife to score it in even lines every centimetre or so. Rub with 1 tablespoon of salt, massaging it well into every scored cut, then leave in the fridge until needed.

Place the celery, onions, garlic, 2 sprigs of the tarragon, the lentils and the wine in the slow cooker dish and mix well. Do not season. Place the pork, skin side up, in a single layer on top of the vegetables. Cover with the lid and cook on low for 6 hours or until the vegetables are soft.

Preheat the grill to its highest setting. If your slow cooker dish is happy under the grill (check the manufacturer's instructions), grill the pork still in the slow cooker dish for 5–10 minutes or until well browned, puffed up and crispy. Alternatively, transfer the pork from the slow cooker dish to a grill tray and cook the pork under the grill. Remove the grilled pork and place on a wooden board or warm serving plate.

Roughly chop the reserved tarragon and mix into the lentils. Season to taste. Serve with slices of pork on top and the cooking juices drizzled over.

Shoulder of pork with fennel and pears

PREPARATION TIME: 10 MINUTES
COOKING TIME: 8–9 HOURS
SERVES 4–6

Shoulder of pork can be a little fatty but slow cooking allows the fat to melt into the meat, giving it loads of extra flavour and succulence.

1.2kg (2lb 12oz) rolled shoulder of pork (bone removed)
2 tbsp fennel seeds
1 tsp sea salt

3 tbsp Dijon mustard
150ml (5fl oz) dry perry or cider
2 pears, peeled, cored and cut into quarters

Dry the surface of the pork with kitchen paper. Roughly crush the fennel seeds and salt together in a mortar with a pestle to release some of their flavour.

Spread the mustard over the fat on the top of the meat and press the fennel salt on top of the mustard layer. Place the meat in the slow cooker dish.

Pour the cider around the meat, being careful not to splash the fennel topping, then place the pears around the meat.

Cover with the lid and cook on low for 8–9 hours. Remove the pork from the slow cooker dish and carve into thick slices. Serve with some pear pieces and cooking juices spooned over, accompanied by creamy mash and freshly cooked seasonal vegetables.

TRY...
using pork chops instead of the rolled shoulder of pork and cook on high for 3 hours.

Baked gammon with roasted root vegetables and cider

PREPARATION TIME: 15 MINUTES

COOKING TIME: 6–9 HOURS

SERVES 4–6

Gammon cooks wonderfully in the slow cooker, leaving it moist and succulent. Here, a joint is cooked on a bed of root vegetables and cider for a perfect one-pot meal.

150g (5oz) baby carrots, scrubbed

2 parsnips, peeled and cored

1 fennel bulb, trimmed

1 red onion, peeled

300ml (10fl oz) cider

Sea salt and freshly ground black
  pepper

1kg (2¼lb) gammon joint

1 tbsp wholegrain mustard

1 tbsp clear honey

2 tbsp roughly chopped fresh
  flat leaf parsley

Place the baby carrots in the slow cooker dish. Cut the parsnips into 1cm (½in) wide wedges, then cut them again to make the pieces about 4cm (1½in) long. Cut the fennel and onion into thin wedges about the same thickness. Add them to the slow cooker dish together with the cider. Season generously with salt and pepper.

Place the gammon on top of the vegetables. Rub the mustard over the fat and drizzle with the honey. Cover with the lid and cook on low for 6–9 hours or until the meat is tender.

Remove the meat from the slow cooker dish and set aside on a board. Mix the parsley into the vegetables, then, using a slotted spoon, place them onto warm plates. Top with a thick slice of gammon and drizzle over the cooking juices.

TRY...

using a pork shoulder or leg joint.

SWEET THINGS

Slow cooking works wonders for desserts and baking. Try these simple recipes for delicious puddings in 2–3 hours.

Winter fruit salad

PREPARATION TIME: 10 MINUTES

COOKING TIME: 2 HOURS

SERVES 4–6   VEGETARIAN

This warm fruit salad is great on its own or as an accompaniment to another dessert. The grenadine gives the fruit a wonderful colour and flavour. You can buy it from most supermarkets, drink specialists or from online suppliers.

300ml (10fl oz) grenadine

450ml (15fl oz) cold water

50g (2oz) caster sugar

1 vanilla pod, split lengthways

3 pears, quartered and cored

4 seasonal eating apples, quartered and cored

6 plums, quartered and stoned

100g (3½oz) blackberries, fresh or frozen

Place the grenadine, cold water, sugar and vanilla pod in the slow cooker dish and add the pears, apples and plums. Cover with a layer of greaseproof paper to ensure that the fruit is completely immersed in the liquid and can't pop above the surface.

Cover with the lid and cook on low for 2 hours or until the fruit is tender when tested with the tip of a knife. Mix in the blackberries and leave to stand for 5 minutes.

Using a slotted spoon, transfer the fruit into a serving dish. Pour the cooking liquid into a pan, bring to the boil over a high heat and boil vigorously for 5–10 minutes or until reduced by half. Serve the poached fruit warm or cold with ice cream or cream and the thickened sauce spooned over.

WHAT ABOUT...

if you want to use the oven? Place all the ingredients in an ovenproof baking dish and cook in an oven preheated to 150°C (300°F), Gas mark 2 for 50 minutes or until the fruit is softened.

Green tea and apple compote

PREPARATION TIME: 5 MINUTES

COOKING TIME: 2–3 HOURS

SERVES 4   VEGETARIAN

This simple fruit purée is lightly scented with green tea and is great served with yogurt, cream or crème fraîche, as an accompaniment to other desserts, or frozen and used as a granita – the choice is yours!

100g (3½oz) unsalted butter

750g (1lb 10oz) eating apples,
  such as Granny Smith

100g (3½oz) caster sugar

2 green tea bags

50ml (1¾fl oz) cold water

Place the butter in the slow cooker dish and turn on to high while you prepare the apples.

Peel, core and roughly chop the apples. Add to the now melted butter and mix well to coat. Add the sugar, tea bags and cold water and fold in.

Cover with the lid and cook for 2–3 hours, stirring occasionally, until thick. If the texture is still a little runny remove the lid and continue cooking until the desired consistency is reached.

Remove the tea bags and discard. Spoon the compote into a blender and blitz until smooth, then if you have time, pass it through a sieve to make it ultra smooth. Serve immediately or cover and chill until needed, allowing it to come up to room temperature again before serving.

WHAT ABOUT...

if you want to cook this on the hob? Cook in a large saucepan over a low heat for about 1 hour then continue from step 4.

Rose-scented rice pudding

PREPARATION TIME: 5 MINUTES
COOKING TIME: 3–4 HOURS
SERVES 8   VEGETARIAN

A rich creamy rice pudding is cooked perfectly in the slow cooker. Here, it's delicately scented with a touch of rose water – if you don't like the rose flavour, just leave it out!

100g (3½oz) butter

125g (4½oz) caster sugar

1.3 litres (2¼ pints) whole milk

1 vanilla pod, split lengthways

A pinch of salt

300g (10oz) pudding rice

A few drops of rose water, or to taste

Roughly chopped pistachios, for sprinkling

Mix all of the ingredients except the rose water and pistachios together in the slow cooker dish.

Cover with the lid and cook on high for 3–4 hours, stirring occasionally, until the rice is tender and creamy.

Add the rose water very sparingly to taste and mix in. Remove the vanilla pod and discard or wash and save for use in another recipe. Sprinkle the pistachios over the top of the rice pudding and serve with a spoonful of poached fruit or a few unsprayed, edible rose petals.

WHAT ABOUT...

if you want to use the oven? Cover with buttered foil and bake in an oven preheated to 180°C (350°F), Gas mark 4 for 60–80 minutes.

Pears poached with Amaretto and vanilla

PREPARATION TIME: 5 MINUTES

COOKING TIME: 4–6 HOURS

SERVES 6   VEGETARIAN

The slow cooker is perfect for poaching fruit as it is a very gentle form of cooking and will stop the fruit breaking up and disintegrating.

6 medium pears

Juice of 1 lemon

2 tbsp caster sugar

100ml (3½ fl oz) Amaretto liqueur

About 500ml (18fl oz) cold water

1 vanilla pod, split lengthways

Using a small paring knife, carefully remove the core from the base of each pear, then peel the pears leaving the stalks intact. Place them in the slow cooker dish and sprinkle with the lemon juice, carefully turning the fruit until it is well coated in the juice.

Sprinkle with the sugar and add the Amaretto, enough cold water to cover the pears and the vanilla pod, then place a piece of greaseproof paper over the fruit to keep it immersed in the liquid.

Cover with the lid and cook on low for 4–6 hours or until the pears are completely tender when tested with the tip of a small sharp knife.

Remove the fruit with a slotted spoon. Strain the poaching liquid into a small pan and warm over a high heat. Bring to the boil and leave to boil vigorously until the liquid is reduced by about half, or until thick and syrupy. Serve the fruit hot or cold with the syrup drizzled over.

TRY...

This is also fantastic with halved, stoned, unpeeled apricots.

Caramelised peaches with basil cream

PREPARATION TIME: 5 MINUTES
COOKING TIME: 2–3 HOURS
SERVES 6   VEGETARIAN

These soft caramelised peaches are fabulous with this delicate, subtly flavoured basil cream.

6 just ripe peaches

50g (2oz) caster sugar

4 tbsp sweet dessert wine (keep
  the rest of the bottle to serve
  with dessert)

300ml (10fl oz) single cream

6 basil leaves

Using a sharp knife, cut the peaches in half and remove the stones, then dip the cut side of the fruit into the sugar to coat.

Place the fruit cut side down in the slow cooker dish and drizzle with the wine. Cover with the lid and cook on low for 2–3 hours or until soft and starting to caramelise.

Meanwhile, pour the cream into a small saucepan and warm over a low heat, stirring occasionally to make sure that it is not sticking to the base of the pan. Do not allow to boil, but when hot, remove from the heat. Add the basil leaves and set aside to cool completely.

Remove the basil from the cream and discard. Serve the peaches cut side up with the cream spooned over and a crisp biscuit on the side.

TRY...
This is great with other seasonal stone fruit too.

Blueberry and lime loaf cake

PREPARATION TIME: 10 MINUTES

COOKING TIME: 3–3½ HOURS

SERVES 4   VEGETARIAN

This simple cake is fabulously light and full of flavour, and it also looks great. Blueberries work brilliantly with the lime but raspberries, blackberries and loganberries also work well too.

100g (3½oz) butter, softened, plus extra for greasing

100g (3½oz) golden caster sugar

2 medium eggs, beaten

50g (2oz) self-raising flour, sifted

50g (2oz) ground almonds

½ tsp baking powder

4 tbsp semi-skimmed milk

Finely grated zest of 1 lime

100g (3½oz) blueberries

Butter a non-stick 500g (1lb) loaf tin and line the base with parchment paper. Place an upturned saucer or trivet into the slow cooker dish and pour enough cold water around it to just cover the top (about 250ml/9fl oz).

Cream the butter and sugar together in a large mixing bowl until light and fluffy. Slowly add the eggs, beating well between each addition. Fold in the flour, almonds and baking powder, then slowly stir in the milk and the lime zest.

Place enough blueberries in the base of the tin to just cover the bottom. Fold the remainder into the sponge mixture, then spoon the sponge into the tin and level the surface with the back of the spoon.

Place the tin in the slow cooker on top of the saucer or trivet and cover with the lid. Cook on high for 3–3½ hours or until risen and spongy to the touch.

Remove the tin from the slow cooker and leave to stand for a minute or so before turning out. Run a sharp knife around the sponge before inverting and leaving to cool completely on a wire rack. Using a serrated knife, cut into thick slices and serve with lashings of cream.

WHAT ABOUT...

if you want to use the oven? Bake this cake in an oven preheated to 170°C (325°F), Gas mark 3 for 50 minutes or until spongy to the touch.

Baileys bread and butter pudding

PREPARATION TIME: 30 MINUTES
COOKING TIME: 2–3 HOURS
SERVES 6   VEGETARIAN

Fruit or no fruit in bread and butter pudding? Purists will adore this fruitless pudding with layers of buttery brioche floating in a rich Baileys-flavoured custard.

12 large slices brioche

Butter, for greasing

150ml (5fl oz) whole milk

200ml (7fl oz) double cream

100ml (3½fl oz) Baileys

75g (3oz) caster sugar

2 eggs

1 egg yolk

6 tsp demerara sugar

Use a 200ml (7fl oz) ramekin to stamp out 24 circles of brioche and set aside. Butter 6 x 200ml (7fl oz) ramekins and divide the brioche rounds among the ramekins in layers.

Whisk the milk, cream, Baileys, caster sugar, eggs and yolk together in a bowl. Pour the custard mixture slowly over the brioche, giving it a chance to soak in between each addition.

Place the ramekins in the slow cooker dish and carefully pour enough boiling water around them to come about halfway up the sides of the dishes. Cover with the lid and cook on high for 2–3 hours or until just firm.

Remove the ramekins from the water bath and scatter with the demerara sugar before serving.

TRY...
adding some raisins or sultanas. Sprinkle about 50g (2oz) of fruit between the brioche layers.

Cherry clafoutis

PREPARATION TIME: 15 MINUTES
COOKING TIME: 2–3 HOURS
SERVES 6   VEGETARIAN

A wonderful dessert prepared quickly and simply and then left to its own devices in the slow cooker. The English cherry season is so short and lacking in supply that this recipe uses a jar of cherries, but do use fresh stoned cherries if you can get them.

700g (1lb 9oz) jar of cherries in natural juice or brandy
50g (2oz) butter, plus extra for greasing
4 medium eggs

2 egg yolks
125g (4½oz) caster sugar
75g (3oz) plain flour, sifted
600ml (1 pint) whole milk

Drain the cherries in a sieve or colander, reserving the juice or brandy that they have been stored in.

Remove the slow cooker dish from the base and preheat the base on high. Butter the slow cooker dish, then scatter the cherries over the base of the dish.

Melt the butter in a small saucepan over a medium heat, then remove from the heat and allow to cool slightly. In a large mixing bowl, mix the eggs with the yolks and sugar.

Whisk in the cooled melted butter, followed by the flour and the milk until smooth, then pour over the cherries.

Place the slow cooker dish in the preheated base and cover with the lid. Cook for 2–3 hours or until just set in the centre. Pour the reserved juice or brandy into a small pan and bring to the boil over a high heat. Cook until it is reduced by about half, then serve drizzled over the clafoutis.

WHAT ABOUT...

if you want to use the oven? Place in a baking dish and bake in an oven preheated to 190°C (375°F), Gas mark 5 for 45–50 minutes or until golden brown and just set.

Rhubarb and custard pots

PREPARATION TIME: 15 MINUTES

COOKING TIME: 3–4 HOURS, PLUS PREHEATING

SERVES 6   VEGETARIAN

A winning combination made even better with slow cooking. The slow poaching of the fruit coaxes out the wonderful flavour of the rhubarb, while the moist conditions in the slow cooker create a wonderfully light custard.

A knob of butter, for greasing

200g (7oz) rhubarb, cut into 2cm (¾in) pieces

25g (1oz) caster sugar, plus extra to taste

Finely grated zest and juice of 1 orange

For the custard:

2 eggs

2 egg yolks

500ml (18fl oz) double cream

75g (3oz) golden caster sugar

Butter the slow cooker dish and add the rhubarb. Add 25g (1oz) of the sugar and the orange zest and juice. Cover with the lid and cook on low for 1–2 hours or until soft. Add more sugar to taste and set aside for several hours to cool completely.

Preheat the slow cooker by turning it on high and butter 6 x 200ml (7fl oz) ovenproof ramekins. Divide the cooled rhubarb mixture between the dishes.

Put the eggs and yolks into a 1 litre (1¾ pint) measuring jug and whisk well. Mix in the cream and sugar, then pour the custard mixture into the dishes.

Place the ramekins in the slow cooker dish and carefully pour enough boiling water around the outside to come about halfway up the sides of the dishes. Cover with the lid and cook on high for 2 hours. Remove the ramekins from the water bath and leave to stand on a heatproof surface for 5 minutes before serving.

Sweet orange and ricotta cheese cakes

PREPARATION TIME: 10 MINUTES

COOKING TIME: 2–3 HOURS

SERVES 6   VEGETARIAN

Light, fluffy, more-ish – and very easy to make.

Butter, for greasing

1 orange

50ml (1¾fl oz) brandy

50g (2oz) sultanas

Seeds from 6 cardamom pods,
  slightly crushed

350g (12oz) ricotta cheese

2 tsp cornflour, sifted

3 large eggs

100g (3½oz) caster sugar

Icing sugar, for dusting

Butter 6 x 200ml (7fl oz) ramekins. Finely grate the zest from the orange and set aside.

Place the brandy, sultanas, juice of the orange and the cardamom seeds into a saucepan and bring to the boil over a high heat. Reduce the heat and simmer for 5 minutes. Allow to cool slightly.

Whisk the ricotta, cornflour, eggs and caster sugar together with the reserved orange zest. Add the cooled sultana mixture and any remaining liquid from the pan.

Pour the mixture into the prepared ramekins, filling them to the very top and place them in the slow cooker dish. Carefully pour enough boiling water around the outside to come about one-third of the way up the sides of the dishes.

Cover with the lid and cook on high for 2–3 hours or until risen and just set. Remove and allow to cool for a couple of minutes before serving, hot or cold, dusted with icing sugar and with dollops of crème fraîche on the side.

TRY...
using a lemon or lime instead of the orange.

Plum and ginger puddings

PREPARATION TIME: 15 MINUTES
COOKING TIME: 2–3 HOURS
SERVES 8   VEGETARIAN

These dainty little puddings are warming and comforting to eat but remarkably light. Serve with ginger syrup, but the custard, cream or ice cream should also always be close to hand!

150g (5oz) butter, softened, plus extra for greasing

175g (6oz) dark brown soft sugar

3 eggs, beaten

150g (5oz) self-raising flour

3 pieces stem ginger in syrup

4 plums, halved and stoned

Cut 8 squares of foil, about 15 x 15cm (6 x 6in) in size. Butter one side of the foil and 8 mini pudding basins. Line the base of each basin with a small square of parchment paper and save the foil for later.

Beat 150g (5oz) of the sugar with the butter in a large mixing bowl with an electric mixer until very pale and fluffy. Gradually add the eggs and then the flour. Strain the stem ginger, reserving about 3 tablespoons of the syrup. Dice the ginger according to taste – either finely or in larger pieces if preferred.

Sprinkle the reserved sugar onto a plate and dip the cut side of each of the plum halves into the sugar to coat thickly. Press each one, cut side down, into the base of each basin.

Divide the cake mixture among the 8 basins and level the surface of each one. Cover the basins tightly with the prepared foil squares and place in the slow cooker dish. Carefully pour enough boiling water around them to come about halfway up the sides of the basins. Cover with the lid and cook on high for 2–3 hours or until the sponge feels springy to the touch.

Remove the basins from the slow cooker and leave to rest for 2–3 minutes. Use a sharp knife to loosen the edge of each sponge, then turn out. Drizzle with the reserved ginger syrup and serve with spoonfuls of crème fraîche.

Cardamom crème brûlée

PREPARATION TIME: 15 MINUTES, PLUS INFUSING
COOKING TIME: 2–3 HOURS, PLUS CHILLING
SERVES 4   VEGETARIAN

Cardamom is a wonderfully fragrant, warming spice, and it works amazingly in this easy but sophisticated brûlée.

568ml tub double cream
3 cardamom pods, crushed
6 egg yolks
7 tbsp golden caster sugar

Warm the cream and cardamom pods over a low heat to just below boiling point. Remove from the heat and set aside for 30 minutes to infuse.

Return the pan to the heat and warm again to just below boiling point. Whisk the egg yolks and 3 tablespoons of the sugar together in a large bowl, then slowly whisk the hot cream into the egg mixture, whisking constantly to prevent the eggs from scrambling.

Strain the custard through a sieve into a large jug, then pour into 4 x 200ml (7fl oz) ramekins. Place the dishes in the slow cooker dish and carefully pour enough boiling water around them to come about halfway up the sides of the ramekins.

Cover with the lid and cook on high for 2–3 hours or until just firm. Remove the ramekins from the slow cooker and leave to cool completely, then cover and chill in the fridge for at least 2 hours, but preferably overnight.

Preheat the grill to its highest setting. Sprinkle the remaining caster sugar over the top of each custard and place under the grill for 3–5 minutes or until the sugar is golden. Remove from the grill and leave for 1 minute before serving.

TRY...
using 2 star anise instead of the cardamom.

Marsala crème caramel

PREPARATION TIME: 20 MINUTES

COOKING TIME: 2–3 HOURS, PLUS PREHEATING AND CHILLING

SERVES 4–6   VEGETARIAN

This retro favourite is always a winner. Here, it's given a little grown-up kick with the addition of some Marsala.

175g (6oz) caster sugar

2 tbsp cold water

For the custard:

150ml (5fl oz) whole milk

275ml (10fl oz) single cream

4 large eggs

1 tsp vanilla extract

2 tbsp good-quality Marsala

Preheat the slow cooker base on high, keeping the dish separate. Place the sugar in a saucepan over a medium heat and leave for about 4–6 minutes or until the sugar begins to dissolve and becomes liquid around the edges. Do not stir but swirl the pan to disperse the sugar, then return it to the heat for a further 2–3 minutes until all the sugar has dissolved and is a dark honey colour.

Remove the pan from the heat and carefully add the cold water, being aware that it may splutter slightly. Return the pan to the heat again and stir until all the caramel is liquid. Pour about two-thirds of the mixture into a heatproof 900ml (1½ pint) dish, about 13 x 10cm (5 x 4in) in size that will fit into your slow cooker dish. Tilt the dish slightly to coat the base and sides with the caramel.

Pour the milk and cream into the pan with the remaining caramel and warm over a low heat, whisking to combine. Break the eggs into a large bowl and whisk lightly, then slowly pour the warm cream mixture over the eggs, whisking constantly to prevent the eggs scrambling. Add the vanilla and Marsala and whisk in.

Place the caramel-lined dish into the slow cooker dish and slot into the preheated base. Pour the cream mixture through a sieve into the dish.

Carefully pour enough boiling water around the outside to come about halfway up the sides of the dish, cover with the lid and cook for 2–3 hours or until just set in the centre – it should still wobble in the middle.

Remove from the cooker and allow to cool completely, then cover and chill for at least 6 hours or preferably overnight. When you're ready to serve, loosen it around the sides with a palette knife and invert onto a deep serving plate. Serve with poached or fresh fruit and a little more cream.

TRY...
using a different liqueur such as Cointreau, brandy or rum instead of the Marsala, if you prefer.

Slow-poached strawberries with Pimm's and clotted cream

PREPARATION TIME: 5 MINUTES
COOKING TIME: 1–2 HOURS
SERVES 4   VEGETARIAN

Combine three classic summer ingredients to make this stunningly simple dessert.

800g (1lb 12oz) strawberries, washed and hulled
100g (3½oz) caster sugar, or to taste

200ml (7fl oz) Pimm's
100ml (3½ fl oz) cold water

Place the strawberries in the slow cooker dish and add the sugar, Pimm's and cold water. Cover with the lid and cook on low for 1–2 hours or until the strawberries are very soft but still holding their shape.

Serve the strawberries topped with dollops of clotted cream and a crisp biscuit or two on the side.

TRY...
using other summer fruits and berries in season.

Banoffee cake

PREPARATION TIME: 10 MINUTES

COOKING TIME: 6–8 HOURS

SERVES 6   VEGETARIAN

Banoffee toffee with caramelised bananas cooked with light golden sponge – great as a pudding or as a cake with morning coffee.

397g tin sweetened condensed milk

100g (3½oz) butter, softened, plus extra for greasing

2 large just ripe bananas, peeled and cut into 2cm (¾in) pieces

100g (3½oz) golden caster sugar

2 medium eggs

100g (3½oz) self-raising flour

1 tsp baking powder

Place the unopened tin of condensed milk into the slow cooker dish and carefully pour over enough boiling water to immerse the tin completely. Cover with the lid and cook on high for 3–4 hours.

Using a thick tea towel, carefully remove the tin from the water and set aside to cool (you can do this up to 2 weeks in advance and keep the cooled tin in the fridge until needed). When completely cool, open the tin, being prepared for some of the contents to try to escape! The milk will have caramelised and turned into a thick golden toffee mixture.

Butter a non-stick 1kg (2¼lb) loaf tin and line the base with parchment paper. Place the bananas in neat rows, cut side down in the prepared tin, then spoon the caramelised toffee over the top to cover completely.

Place the butter, sugar, eggs, flour and baking powder in a food processor and blitz until smooth. Spoon over the toffee layer in the tin and level the surface. Cover tightly with buttered foil.

Place the tin in the slow cooker dish and carefully pour enough boiling water around the outside to come about halfway up the sides of the tin. Cover with the lid and cook on high for 3–4 hours or until soft and spongy. Allow to cool for 5–10 minutes, then invert onto a serving plate. Serve with lightly whipped cream.

Rich chocolate and hazelnut cake

PREPARATION TIME: 20 MINUTES

COOKING TIME: 3–4 HOURS, PLUS PREHEATING AND COOLING

MAKES AN 18CM (7IN) CAKE   VEGETARIAN

Chocolate, roasted hazelnuts, chocolaty sponge – perfection!

- 150g (5oz) butter, softened, plus extra for greasing
- 125g (4½oz) caster sugar
- 2 large eggs, beaten
- 100g (3½oz) self-raising flour
- 25g (1oz) cocoa powder
- 2 tbsp whole milk, as needed
- 100g (3½oz) roasted hazelnuts, finely chopped
- 150g (5oz) plain dark chocolate, roughly chopped

Preheat the slow cooker on high. Butter an 18cm (7in) deep springform cake tin that fits into your slow cooker dish and line the base with parchment paper.

Beat 125g (4½oz) of the butter and the sugar together in a large mixing bowl with an electric mixer until light and fluffy. Gradually add the eggs, beating well between each addition. Sift in the flour and cocoa and fold in until combined and drops easily from the spoon. Add milk if the mixture is too thick. Fold in 75g (3oz) of the nuts and 75g (3oz) of the chocolate, then spoon into the prepared tin and level the surface. Cover with a double layer of parchment paper and foil and seal well, leaving enough room for the cake to rise.

Place the tin in the slow cooker dish and pour enough boiling water around the outside to come about one-third of the way up the side of the tin. Cover with the lid and cook for 3–4 hours or until springy to the touch.

Remove the tin from the slow cooker and leave for 5 minutes before unwrapping. Turn out onto a wire rack and allow to cool.

Melt the remaining chocolate in a heatproof bowl set over a pan of just simmering water. Once melted, allow to cool, slightly then beat in the remaining softened butter to combine. Spread over the cake evenly and scatter the remaining nuts over the top before serving in large slices.

Blackberry and apple roly-poly

PREPARATION TIME: 20–25 MINUTES

COOKING TIME: 2–3 HOURS

SERVES 6–8

This roly-poly should not be relegated to winter – it has a very light texture and the addition of lemon zest makes it rather zingy too.

150g (5oz) fresh blackberries

1 eating apple, peeled, cored and diced

1 tbsp icing sugar

Butter, for greasing

300g (10oz) self-raising flour, plus extra for dusting

150g (5oz) shredded suet

75g (3oz) caster sugar

Finely grated zest of 1 lemon

175–200ml (6–7fl oz) whole milk

Cold water or milk, for brushing

To make the filling, warm the blackberries, apple and icing sugar together in a saucepan over a medium heat until the fruits begin to soften. Increase the heat, bring to the boil and cook for 5–10 minutes or until the juices thicken and become jammy. Pour the mixture into a bowl and leave to cool.

Butter and lightly flour a large sheet of parchment paper, about 40 x 30cm (16 x 12 in), and place it on a larger sheet of foil.

To make the dough, mix the flour, suet, caster sugar and lemon zest together in a large bowl. Stir in enough milk until the mixture forms a soft dough, then gather together into a ball, but don't overwork or knead it as it will become tough.

On a lightly floured surface, roll the dough into a rectangle about 22 x 25cm (8¹/₂ x 10in). Spread with the cooled blackberry mixture, leaving a 2cm (³/₄in) border around the edge, and moisten the border with a little cold water or milk. Starting from one of the shorter ends of dough, begin rolling into a tight cylinder. With the seam underneath, lay the roly-poly in the centre of the parchment paper. Fold over the long paper and foil edges to seal, leaving enough space above the pudding to allow it to rise. Squeeze the paper ends together tightly to seal them.

Scrunch a large piece of foil into a thick cushion about the same size as the roly-poly and place this in the base of the slow cooker dish. Lay the parcel on top and carefully pour enough boiling water around it to just cover the foil cushion and come to the base of the roly-poly. Cover with the lid and cook on high for 2–3 hours or until firm to the touch.

Remove from the slow cooker and leave to rest for a minute or two before unwrapping. Use a serrated knife to cut it into thick slices and serve immediately with vanilla custard.

Marzipan-baked apples

PREPARATION TIME: 10 MINUTES
COOKING TIME: 3–4 HOURS
SERVES 4   VEGETARIAN

Baked apples are so redolent of cold autumnal days. The slow cooker makes the most of the apple flavour by allowing it to develop gradually without the apples overcooking, while the marzipan stuffing flavours them from within.

4 medium Bramley cooking apples
25g (1oz) dates, chopped
25g (1oz) walnut pieces
50g (2oz) soft light brown sugar

50g (2oz) natural golden marzipan, softened
A large pinch of mixed spice
4 tbsp cold water

Using a corer, remove the core from each of the apples, then, using a small sharp knife, lightly score a horizontal line around the middle of each apple.

Mix the remaining ingredients, except the cold water, in a bowl using the back of a wooden spoon to blend everything together. Divide the mixture evenly among the holes in the apples, pressing it down until it is all used up.

Stand the apples in the slow cooker dish and add the cold water. Cover with the lid and cook on low for 3–4 hours or until the apples are soft and the filling is hot. Serve with any cooking juices drizzled over and plenty of cream or custard.

Gooey chocolate pudding

PREPARATION TIME: 15 MINUTES
COOKING TIME: 2–3 HOURS, PLUS PREHEATING
SERVES 6–8   VEGETARIAN

This pudding is rich and dark with a soft molten centre as long as it's not overcooked, when it will revert back to being a chocolate sponge. So, for the best results, serve it while the middle is still wobbly and gooey . This pudding is great served with crème fraîche and summer berries.

75g (3oz) unsalted butter, plus
  extra for greasing
100g (3½oz) plain dark chocolate,
  broken into pieces
100g (3½oz) self-raising flour
100g (3½oz) ground almonds
50g (2oz) caster sugar

A pinch of salt
2 large eggs
2 egg yolks
175ml (6fl oz) whole milk
100g (3½oz) white chocolate, cut
  into chunks

Remove the slow cooker dish and preheat the slow cooker base on high. Butter the inside of the dish liberally. Place the plain dark chocolate in a heatproof bowl set over a saucepan of simmering water and leave to melt. Make sure the bowl doesn't touch the water.

Sift the flour and almonds into a large bowl, add half of the sugar, the salt, eggs, yolks and milk and whisk until smooth.

Add the remaining butter to the now melted chocolate and mix well. Leave until the butter has melted completely, then slowly pour the melted chocolate and butter into the egg mixture, whisking as you go. Fold in the white chocolate.

Pour the mixture into the slow cooker dish, place it in the preheated cooker base and cover with the lid. Cook for 2–3 hours or until set around the edges but still wobbly in the centre. Remove the slow cooker dish from the base and leave to stand for 5 minutes before serving.

Syrup pudding

PREPARATION TIME: 10 MINUTES

COOKING TIME: 3–4 HOURS, PLUS PREHEATING

SERVES 4

The old ones are always the best! This is a simple unadulterated recipe, which couldn't be better suited to the slow cooker.

Butter, for greasing	50g (2oz) caster sugar
4 tbsp golden syrup	50g (2oz) shredded suet
100g (3½oz) self-raising flour	1 egg, beaten
A pinch of salt	2 tbsp milk

Preheat the slow cooker on high and butter a 600ml (1 pint) pudding basin. Spoon in the golden syrup.

Mix the flour, salt and sugar together in a large mixing bowl, add the suet and rub in lightly with your fingertips to incorporate into the flour slightly. Gradually mix in the beaten egg and milk until well combined and the mixture is thick and smooth.

Spoon the mixture into the basin and cover with a double layer of parchment paper and foil, leaving plenty of room for the pudding to rise, but securing it tightly around the edges.

Place into the slow cooker dish and carefully pour enough boiling water around the outside to come about halfway up the sides of the dish. Cover with the lid and cook for 3–4 hours or until springy to the touch.

Remove from the slow cooker and leave to cool for 5 minutes before unwrapping. Use the tip of a sharp knife to loosen the edges of the pudding before inverting it onto a serving plate to turn out – be careful, the syrup will be hot and will attempt to escape around the edges. Serve hot with plenty of custard.

TRY...

using jam or marmalade instead of the golden syrup.

Lemon upside-down pudding

PREPARATION TIME: 20 MINUTES
COOKING TIME: 1½ HOURS
SERVES 6   VEGETARIAN

There are so many variations of this recipe in existence – this one is a family hand-me-down relied on frequently for Sunday lunches over the generations. Here, it adapts amazingly to slow cooking, producing a particularly light sponge floating on a pool of dreamy, zingy lemon custard – a conventional oven should never be used for this recipe again!

100g (3½oz) butter, softened	4 eggs, separated
175g (6oz) caster sugar	50g (2oz) plain flour
3 lemons	500ml (18fl oz) semi-skimmed milk

Butter a 2 litre (3½ pint) shallow baking dish just a little smaller than the slow cooker dish with some of the butter. Place the rest in a bowl, add the sugar and mix with an electric whisk until pale and fluffy.

Finely grate the zest from 2 of the lemons and add it to the blended butter and sugar, then add the juice of all 3 lemons. Mix everything together – don't worry, the mixture should curdle at this point.

Mix in the egg yolks and flour, followed by the milk to make a runny batter. In a clean bowl, using clean utensils, whisk the egg whites until firm, then fold them gently into the batter.

Place the prepared dish in the slow cooker dish and pour enough cold water around the outside until it comes about halfway up the sides. Pour the lemon mixture into the prepared dish. Cover with the lid and cook on high for 1½ hours or until just set but still wobbly in the centre.

Carefully remove the dish and serve immediately with dollops of crème fraîche, if you like.

TRY...
using limes instead of lemons, or a mixture of both, if you prefer.

Boozy Christmas pudding

PREPARATION TIME: 20 MINUTES
COOKING TIME: 8–10 HOURS, PLUS REHEATING
SERVES 4–6

Everyone seems to have a family recipe for the best Christmas pudding. Why not try a new one this year – you never know this one might become your new favourite! Whichever you choose, the slow cooker makes really easy work of the whole process, making the worry of the pan boiling dry a non-existent issue! Make this pudding about 6–8 weeks before Christmas.

Butter, for greasing
100g (3½oz) golden caster sugar
100g (3½oz) shredded suet
175g (6oz) sultanas
175g (6oz) raisins
100g (3½oz) currants
50g (2oz) plain flour
50g (2oz) fresh white breadcrumbs
25g (1oz) flaked almonds
Finely grated zest of 1 orange
½ tsp ground cinnamon

½ tsp mixed spice
½ tsp freshly grated nutmeg
A small pinch of salt
2 large eggs, beaten
75ml (2½fl oz) brandy or rum, plus extra for feeding

Preheat the slow cooker on high and lightly butter a 1.2 litre (2 pint) pudding basin.

Mix together all the dry ingredients in a large bowl, then stir in the eggs and brandy or rum and mix well.

Spoon the mixture into the prepared basin. Place a round of parchment paper and foil over the top and tie securely with string. Make a string handle from one side of the basin to the other so it is easier to take the basin out of the slow cooker dish after cooking.

Place the basin in the slow cooker dish and carefully pour enough boiling water around the outside to come about halfway up the sides of the basin.

Cover with the lid and cook for 8–10 hours, topping the boiling water up from time to time, if necessary – but you probably won't need to.

Remove the basin from the slow cooker and allow to cool. Change the parchment paper and foil covers for fresh ones and tie up as before. Store in a cool cupboard until Christmas Day, unwrapping and feeding the pudding with a drizzle of brandy or rum each week or two and wrapping up again.

On Christmas Day preheat the slow cooker on high. Return the pudding to the slow cooker dish and surround with boiling water as before. Cover and cook on high for 4 hours or until piping hot throughout. Serve with brandy butter, rum sauce, cream or home-made custard – however you like it.

WHAT ABOUT...

if you want to cook on the hob? Use a steamer or place the basin in a large saucepan with a trivet or inverted heatproof saucer on the base. Pour enough boiling water into the base of the steamer to come one-third of the way up the sides of the basin. Cover and leave to simmer for about 5–6 hours, topping up the water occasionally as necessary.

CHUTNEYS, JAMS AND DRINKS

Combine simple ingredients to
create storecupboard essentials,
gifts and festive drinks.

Apple and mint jelly

PREPARATION TIME: 10 MINUTES, PLUS STRAINING
COOKING TIME: 2–3 HOURS PLUS COOLING
MAKES ABOUT 2KG (4LB 8OZ)   VEGETARIAN

Making your own jelly is very satisfying. Buy jelly bags and muslin from cook shops (online sites have a wide selection).

1.5kg (3lb 5oz) Bramley cooking apples, unpeeled, cored and roughly chopped
25g (1oz) fresh mint, leaves only
1 cinnamon stick
750ml (1¼ pints) cold water

100g (3½oz) chopped baby spinach
300ml (10fl oz) cider vinegar
500g–1kg (1lb 2oz–2¼lb) preserving sugar (see below)

Place a saucer in the freezer ready for testing the jelly. Place the apples in the slow cooker dish with all but about one-quarter of the mint leaves and the cinnamon stick. Add the cold water, cover with the lid and cook on high for about 1 hour, stirring occasionally until soft and thick. Add the spinach, stir to combine, then pour in the cider vinegar. Cook, uncovered, for a further hour. Spoon the mixture into a jelly bag (follow the instructions on the pack) and leave to strain over a bowl overnight – don't be tempted to press this through the muslin; leave until the dripping stops.

Wrap the remaining mint leaves in a small muslin bag. Measure the amount of drained apple and spinach juice and place in a large saucepan. Add 500g (1lb 2oz) of preserving sugar for every 600ml (1 pint) of juice. Discard the pulp in the jelly bag.

Place the pan over a medium heat and stir until the sugar has dissolved. Add the bag of mint, then bring to a rapid boil and leave, boiling away, for 10 minutes or until reduced slightly. Remove from the heat and set aside for a couple of minutes. Dab a spoonful of jelly onto the frozen saucer and leave for 30 seconds before pushing your finger through it. If the surface of the jelly wrinkles it is ready. If not, return to the heat and boil for slightly longer, then re-test. Remove any scum from the surface with a large spoon, then pour into sterilised jars, cover with wax discs and allow to cool.

Shiraz jelly

PREPARATION TIME: 5 MINUTES
COOKING TIME: 3 HOURS PLUS COOLING
MAKES ABOUT 500G (1LB 2OZ)

A perfect accompaniment to hot and cold meats, as well as to an after-dinner cheese board, this jelly also makes a lovely present when packaged up in little jars.

300g (10oz) caster sugar
75cl bottle good-quality Shiraz
  wine

8 cloves
2 fresh thyme sprigs
7 leaves of gelatine

Place the sugar and wine in the slow cooker dish and cook on high for 30 minutes or until the sugar has dissolved.

Add the cloves and thyme leaves, then cover with the lid and cook on high for 1 hour.

Remove the lid and reduce the temperature to low. Cook for a further 2 hours or until reduced slightly. Remove the dish from the slow cooker base.

Place the gelatine in a bowl and cover with cold water. Leave to soak for 5–10 minutes or according to the packet instructions. Remove the leaves and squeeze to release any excess water, then stir into the warm wine.

Strain through a sieve into sterilised jars, cover with wax discs and leave to cool completely. Seal and place in the fridge to set. Use when set or keep in the fridge for up to a month.

TRY...
making other wine jellies in a similar way – Chardonnay works well, as do other robust varieties.

Classic marmalade with whisky

PREPARATION TIME: 15–20 MINUTES
COOKING TIME: 2¼ HOURS PLUS COOLING
MAKES ABOUT 700G (1LB 9OZ)   VEGETARIAN

The slow cooker is perfect for softening up the orange rind when making marmalade.

450g (1lb) oranges (about 4),
  preferably Seville, halved
300ml (10fl oz) cold water

450g (1lb) granulated or jam sugar
2 tbsp whisky

Place a saucer in the freezer to chill. Squeeze the juice from the oranges and place in the slow cooker dish. Reserve the pips, pith and peel.

Using a sharp knife, shred the peel finely into strips about 1cm x 3mm (½ x ⅛in) in size. If the pith is very thick, trim some off to a maximum of 5mm (¼in).

Add the peel to the slow cooker dish together with the cold water. Tie the pips and pith in a square of muslin and add as well. Cover with the lid and cook on high for 2 hours or until the peel is very soft.

Tip the mixture into a heavy-based saucepan, add the sugar and heat gently, stirring constantly, until dissolved. Bring to a rapid boil and cook for 15 minutes. Dab a spoonful of marmalade onto the frozen saucer and leave for 30 seconds before pushing your finger through it. If the surface of the mixture wrinkles it is ready. If not, return to the heat and boil for slightly longer, then re-test.

Remove the pan from the heat and lift out the muslin bag with a spoon. Leave to stand for 15 minutes, then stir in the whisky.

Spoon the marmalade into hot sterilised jars and cover with wax discs. Allow to cool, then seal and store in a cool, dry place for up to six months. Once opened, keep in the fridge and use within three weeks.

TRY...
making this on the hob. Use a large saucepan and place over a low heat.

Low-sugar fig and ginger jam

PREPARATION TIME: 10 MINUTES
COOKING TIME: 5–6 HOURS PLUS COOLING
MAKES 1KG (2¼LB)   VEGETARIAN

Jam is usually made with equal quantities of fruit and sugar, but slow cooking enables you to use less sugar, although your jam will be a little runnier than normal.

1kg (2¼lb) fresh figs, stemmed
  and cut into quarters
1 lemon, very finely sliced
500g (1lb 2oz) jam sugar with
  pectin

125ml (4fl oz) cold water
2 tbsp chopped stem ginger

Place a saucer in the freezer to chill. Place the figs and lemon in the slow cooker dish with the sugar, cold water and ginger.

Cover with the lid and cook on low for 2½ hours or until starting to thicken, stirring twice during cooking.

Remove the lid and increase the temperature to high. Cook for a further 2–3 hours or until the jam is thick.

Remove the saucer from the freezer. Take a teaspoon of the jam and place it onto the saucer. Allow to cool slightly for 1–2 minutes, then push a finger lightly through the jam. If the surface wrinkles it is ready. If not, return to the heat and boil for slightly longer, then re-test.

Ladle the jam into sterilised jars, cover with wax discs and allow to cool, then seal and store in the fridge for up to two months.

WHAT ABOUT...

If you can't get fresh figs use the Apricot and Cardamom Jam recipe on page 155, using dried figs in place of the apricots and add some ginger to the mixture instead of cardamom pods.

Low-sugar strawberry and vanilla jam

PREPARATION TIME: 10 MINUTES

COOKING TIME: 5½–6½ HOURS PLUS COOLING

MAKES 1KG (2¼LB)   VEGETARIAN

Normally, jam requires equal quantities of fruit to sugar to set properly, but the slow cooking of this recipe allows the mixture to use less sugar. Your jam won't be as firm as some but you will have used 50 per cent less sugar.

1kg (2¼lb) strawberries	2 tbsp lemon juice
500g (1lb 2oz) jam sugar with	A pinch of sea salt
pectin	1 vanilla pod

Place a saucer into the freezer to chill. Wash and drain the strawberries, then hull. Cut any large fruit into smaller pieces.

Place the strawberries in the slow cooker dish with the sugar, lemon juice and salt. Crush lightly with a potato masher or fork and leave to stand for 15 minutes or until the sugar has dissolved.

Using a small sharp knife, split the vanilla pod in half lengthways and scrape out the seeds. Add these and the pod to the slow cooker dish. Cover with the lid and cook on high for 2½ hours, stirring twice during cooking, until beginning to thicken.

Remove the lid and continue to cook for a further 3–4 hours, stirring occasionally, until thick.

Remove the saucer from the freezer and place a teaspoonful of the jam onto it. Leave for a minute or two and then push an index finger through it. If the surface of the jam wrinkles it is ready. If not, cook for another 30 minutes and re-test. Using a pair of tongs, remove the vanilla pod. Be careful as it will be very hot.

Ladle the jam into sterilised jars, cover with wax discs and allow to cool completely. Seal and store in the fridge and use within two months.

Apricot and cardamom jam

PREPARATION TIME: 10 MINUTES

COOKING TIME: 4½–5½ HOURS PLUS COOLING

MAKES ABOUT 1KG (2¼LB)   VEGETARIAN

This is a bit of a cheat's jam really, but still gives a great result. Cardamom and apricots are a great combination, as the spice just gives the fruit a little edge of fragrance and warmth. This is great with scones or spread in the middle of a Victoria sandwich.

500g (1lb 2oz) dried ready-to-eat apricots

20 cardamom pods

200g (7oz) golden granulated sugar

750ml (1¼ pints) cold water

Place the apricots in a food processor and blitz until finely chopped – if your blender struggles with this add a spoonful or two of water to loosen the mixture.

Using a small sharp knife, cut the cardamom pods open to reveal the small black seeds. Remove the seeds and discard the husks. Add the seeds to the food processor and blitz again to combine.

Spoon the mixture into the slow cooker dish and add the sugar and cold water. Stir well for about 1 minute or until the sugar starts to dissolve, then cover with the lid and cook on high for 2½ hours, stirring twice during cooking, until slightly thickened.

Remove the lid and continue cooking for 2–3 hours, stirring occasionally, until thick. The contents of the slow cooker will be extremely hot so caution should be taken throughout this time.

Ladle into sterilised jars and cover with wax discs. Leave until completely cold then seal and store in the fridge for up to three weeks.

TRY...
using other dried fruit, such as figs, prunes or pears, if you prefer.

Pickled plums

PREPARATION TIME: 10 MINUTES, PLUS MARINATING
COOKING TIME: 10–12 HOURS
MAKES ABOUT 1KG (2¼LB)   VEGETARIAN

This is almost a sauce really and can be served warm or cold. Either way it tastes great, as the slow cooking really concentrates the plums' flavour. Try it with meats, burgers or sausages.

12 just ripe plums
100g (3½oz) caster sugar
Finely grated zest and juice of
  1 orange
Juice of 1 lemon

1 tsp pickling spice
½ cinnamon stick
1 green chilli, deseeded and finely
  diced
1 tbsp red wine vinegar

Mix all of the ingredients together in a bowl, cover and chill for at least 12 hours or preferably overnight.

When the plums have marinated, pour the contents of the bowl into the slow cooker dish. Cover with the lid and cook on low for 10–12 hours or until starting to caramelise slightly.

Use the plums warm or pour into sterilised jars and allow to cool, then seal and store in the fridge for up to three weeks.

WHAT ABOUT...
if you want to cook this in the oven? At step 2 pour the contents of the bowl into a roasting tray and cook in an oven preheated to 140°C (275°F), Gas mark 1 for 6–8 hours until caramelised. Remove from the oven and set aside until needed or continue from step 3.

Lime and lemongrass curd

PREPARATION TIME: 5 MINUTES
COOKING TIME: 3–4 HOURS PLUS COOLING
MAKES ABOUT 1KG (2¼LB)   VEGETARIAN

Curds are wonderfully easy to make, but they do need lots of constant attention when being made conventionally. The slow cooker removes the need to watch over the mixture, making it fabulously easy.

Finely grated zest and juice of
  4 limes
1 lemongrass stalk, outer layers
  removed

100g (3½oz) butter
450g (1lb) caster sugar
4 medium eggs

Place the lime zest and juice in a medium-sized saucepan. Using a rolling pin, bash the lemongrass lightly to bruise it, then add it to the pan together with the butter.

Warm the pan over a low-medium heat until the butter has melted, then add the sugar. Remove from the heat and stir until the sugar has dissolved completely. Allow to cool slightly, then remove the lemongrass and discard.

Whisk the eggs in a large heatproof bowl that fits into your slow cooker dish. Gradually whisk in the lime mixture, whisking constantly, then cover the bowl tightly with foil.

Place the bowl in the slow cooker dish and carefully pour enough boiling water around the outside to come about halfway up the sides of the bowl. Cover with the lid and cook on low for 3–4 hours or until thick and glossy.

Beat the mixture well with a wooden spoon until completely smooth, then ladle into sterilised jars and cover with wax discs. Leave to cool, then seal and store in the fridge for up to three weeks.

TRY...
using other citrus fruit, such as oranges or lemons, or a combination of both.

Lime pickle

PREPARATION TIME: 5 MINUTES
COOKING TIME: 8–10 HOURS PLUS COOLING
SERVES 8

VEGETARIAN

An essential accompaniment to curries, lime pickle takes quite a long time to make, needing several days or weeks to marinate in salt. Ironically, in this instance, a slow cooker actually speeds up the process! This is great with poppadums or to accompany a curry.

4 limes, cut into quarters

1 tbsp salt

1 tbsp groundnut oil

3cm (1¼in) piece fresh root ginger, peeled and sliced

1 tbsp white vinegar

1–2 green chillies, finely diced

About 3 tbsp caster sugar

1 tbsp paprika

1 tsp garam masala

1 tsp cumin seeds

2 garlic cloves, peeled and finely sliced

Place the limes in the slow cooker dish with all the remaining ingredients and mix thoroughly.

Cover with the lid and cook on low for 8–10 hours, stirring occasionally, until thickened. If it remains fairly liquid, then remove the lid and cook for a further hour. Add more sugar to taste, although be careful as the mixture will be very hot.

Carefully spoon into sterilised jars and allow to cool, then seal and store in the fridge for a week before eating. It must be eaten within a month.

TRY...
adjusting the seasoning with sugar after cooking to get the best results.

Green chilli jam

PREPARATION TIME: 15 MINUTES
COOKING TIME: 3 HOURS PLUS COOLING
MAKES 250G (9OZ)   VEGETARIAN

A tasty, zingy savoury jam, which is great with cheeses, meats, salads and sausages and particularly good with pork pies.

12 large green chillies

1 onion, peeled and very finely diced

2 garlic cloves, peeled and finely chopped

6cm (2½in) piece fresh root ginger, peeled and finely chopped

100ml (3½fl oz) vegetable oil

2 tsp caster sugar

100ml (3½fl oz) white wine vinegar

1 tbsp Thai fish sauce, to taste

Using a sharp knife, cut the chillies in half lengthways, then deseed and chop the flesh finely.

Place the chillies in the slow cooker dish together with the onion, garlic, ginger, vegetable oil and sugar. Cover with the lid and cook on low for 2 hours, stirring occasionally, until the vegetables have softened and are just starting to caramelise.

Add the vinegar and stir well. Leave uncovered and continue to cook for about 1 hour or until the liquid evaporates slightly.

Mix in the fish sauce to taste. Spoon into sterilised jars, allow to cool, then seal and store in the fridge for up to a month.

TRY...
This is equally good with red chillies, just slightly hotter.

Tomato chutney

PREPARATION TIME: 10 MINUTES
COOKING TIME: 5 HOURS PLUS COOLING
MAKES ABOUT 500G (1LB 2OZ)   VEGETARIAN

If you grow your own, this is a great recipe for using up the glut of summer tomatoes.

1kg (2¼lb) tomatoes, peeled,
  deseeded and chopped
3 tbsp soft light brown sugar
1 tbsp mustard seeds

2 tbsp red wine vinegar
3 tbsp olive oil
Sea salt and freshly ground white
  pepper

Place the tomatoes, sugar, vinegar and olive oil in the slow cooker dish and mix well. Season generously with salt and white pepper.

Cover with the lid and cook on high, stirring occasionally, for 2 hours until the tomatoes are very soft.

Remove the lid and continue cooking for a further 3 hours, stirring occasionally, until thick and jammy.

Pour the chutney into sterilised jars and allow to cool. Seal and store in the fridge for up to a month.

TRY...
adding some dried chilli flakes for a chutney with more of a kick.

Red onion marmalade

PREPERATION TIME: 15 MINUTES

COOKING TIME: 6–8 HOURS PLUS COOLING

MAKES 1KG (2¼LB)   VEGETARIAN

Soft, sticky onion marmalade – great with pâtés (such as the Farmhouse Pâté on page 46) salads or cooked meats like steak and duck.

2kg (4lb 8oz) red onions, peeled, halved and thinly sliced

4 garlic cloves, peeled and thinly sliced

150g (5oz) butter

4 tbsp olive oil

150g (5oz) caster sugar

1 tbsp fresh thyme leaves

A pinch of dried chilli flakes (optional)

Sea salt and freshly ground black pepper

75cl bottle red wine

350ml (12fl oz) sherry vinegar or red wine vinegar

200ml (7fl oz) port

Place the onions and garlic in the slow cooker dish together with the butter and olive oil and mix well to combine. Sprinkle with the sugar, thyme leaves, chilli flakes (if using) and some salt and pepper. Cover with the lid and cook on high, stirring occasionally, for 3–4 hours or until very soft and caramelised.

Add the wine, vinegar and port and cook, uncovered, for a further 3–4 hours, stirring occasionally, until thick and a dark brown colour.

Allow to cool, then spoon into sterilised jars and seal. Eat straight away or store in the fridge for up to three months.

TRY...

making this jam with ordinary brown onions, especially if you have some that need using up.

Sweet and sour pickled onions

PREPARATION TIME: 15 MINUTES

COOKING TIME: 3 HOURS

MAKES 1KG (2¼LB)   VEGETARIAN

If you're a fan of pickled onions you'll love this easy recipe. These onions are great served with cold meats and salads and are rather good in Cheddar cheese sandwiches too.

30 small white onions	1 bay leaf
2 tbsp tomato purée	250ml (9fl oz) dry white wine
100ml (3½fl oz) red wine vinegar	250ml (9fl oz) water
2 tbsp olive oil	100g (3½oz) raisins
2 tbsp caster sugar	200ml (7fl oz) cold water

Place the onions in a large bowl and cover with boiling water. Leave to stand for 5 minutes, then drain and peel off the skins. Place the peeled onions in the slow cooker dish.

Add the remaining ingredients to the slow cooker dish, then cover with the lid and cook on high for 3 hours or until the onions are soft.

Spoon the mixture into sterilised jars. Allow to cool, then seal and store in the fridge for up to three months.

WHAT ABOUT...

if you want to cook on the hob? Place all the ingredients in a large saucepan, cover with a lid and cook over a very low heat for 2–3 hours, checking that the liquid has not evaporated and adding more cold water as required.

Mango chutney

PREPARATION TIME: 15 MINUTES
COOKING TIME: 3–4 HOURS PLUS COOLING
MAKES 1KG (2¼LB)   VEGETARIAN

This chutney is an essential accompaniment to curry and poppadums, but it is also great with strong cheeses and cold meats.

3 firm mangoes, peeled, stoned and cut into 2cm (¾in) pieces
125ml (4fl oz) white wine vinegar
75g (3oz) caster sugar, plus extra to taste
1½ tsp salt, or to taste
50g (2oz) raisins
2cm (¾in) piece fresh root ginger, peeled

1 bird's eye chilli
3 garlic cloves, peeled
1 tsp ground cumin
1 tsp ground coriander seeds
½ tsp turmeric
1 cinnamon stick
2 star anise
1 tbsp kalonji (black onion) seeds
2 tbsp vegetable oil

Place the mangoes in the slow cooker dish and add the vinegar, sugar, salt and raisins.

Place the ginger, chilli, garlic, cumin, coriander and turmeric into a mini blender and blitz to combine into a rough paste.

Add the paste to the mango mixture and mix in together with the cinnamon stick, star anise, kalonji seeds and vegetable oil.

Cover with the lid and cook on low for 3–4 hours or until thickened. Allow to cool, then remove the cinnamon and star anise. Spoon into sterilised jars, cover with wax disks and store in the fridge for up to a month.

WHAT ABOUT...
You can buy *kalonji* (black onion) seeds from good supermarkets or Asian food stores. They are worth purchasing, as they give the chutney a unique and authentic flavour.

Fig chutney

PREPARATION TIME: 10 MINUTES

COOKING TIME: 4–5 HOURS

MAKES 1KG (2¼LB)   VEGETARIAN

This is a simple spiced chutney, which is perfect to accompany cheeses, cured meats and crusty bread.

1kg (2¼lb) fresh figs

350g (12oz) soft dark brown sugar

250ml (9fl oz) cider vinegar

2 tbsp chopped fresh root ginger

Sea salt and freshly ground black
  pepper

1 small onion, peeled and diced

1 tsp black mustard seeds

¼ tsp ground cinnamon

A pinch of ground cloves

Using a sharp knife, trim the stems from the figs and cut the fruit into quarters. Place the sugar, vinegar, ginger, 2 teaspoons of salt, the onion and spices in the slow cooker dish and mix well. Cover with the lid and cook on low for 3 hours.

Season to taste with salt and pepper, adding more spices if necessary. Remove the lid and increase the temperature to high. Cook for a further 1–2 hours or until thickened.

Spoon the mixture into sterilised preserving jars (see tip) and allow to cool. Cover with wax disks and keep in the fridge for up to three months.

WHAT ABOUT...

All jams, preserves, chutneys and relishes must be potted in very clean containers. Wash jars and bottles thoroughly in hot soapy water and dry in a warm oven preheated to 150°C (300°F), Gas mark 2 (make sure you don't put any plastic seals or lids in the oven as they will melt). After drying, handle the jars and bottles as little as possible and leave on a clean tea towel. When the jam or chutney is cooked, pour the hot mixture into the prepared containers while they are still warm – this will lessen the chance of the glass cracking – and fill them almost to the top.

Thai pickled tomatoes

PREPARATION TIME: 15 MINUTES
COOKING TIME: 5½–6½ HOURS PLUS COOLING
MAKES ABOUT 1KG (2¼LB)   VEGETARIAN

Thai food is a wonderful balance between sweet, sour, salty and spicy, and this pickle is no exception. It's great with prawn crackers for nibbles or as a side for main Thai dishes, or equally good with meats and creamy cheeses too.

1–2 bird's eye chillies
3 garlic cloves, peeled and chopped
2.5cm (1in) piece fresh root ginger, peeled and chopped
2 lemongrass stalks, peeled and chopped
1½ tsp turmeric
2½ tbsp sunflower oil
1 large onion, peeled, halved and sliced

250ml (9fl oz) rice or white wine vinegar
125ml (4fl oz) cold water
125g (4½oz) soft brown sugar
3 tbsp fish sauce
800g (1lb 12oz) firm vine-ripened tomatoes, cut into wedges
3 kaffir lime leaves
Sea salt and freshly ground black pepper

Blitz the chillies, garlic, ginger, lemongrass, turmeric and sunflower oil in a food processor until it forms a paste.

Add the paste and the onion to the slow cooker dish, then cover with the lid and cook on high, stirring occasionally, for 2 hours or until the onions are soft and fragrant.

Add the vinegar, cold water, sugar and fish sauce and cook, uncovered, for 30 minutes or until the sugar dissolves completely. Add the tomatoes and lime leaves and mix well.

Cook, uncovered, for a further 3–4 hours or until slightly thickened. Season to taste with salt and pepper and allow to cool to room temperature. Pour into sterilised jars, cover and store in the fridge for up to five days.

Hot chilli sauce

PREPARATION TIME: 10 MINUTES
COOKING TIME: 9–10 HOURS
MAKES ABOUT 900ML (1½ PINTS)   VEGETARIAN

This fiery sauce is fantastic! If you prefer a milder version then reduce the number of chillies and remove the seeds too. This sauce is great with burgers, sausages and anything that needs a bit of a kick!

10 plum tomatoes, peeled

1 tbsp caster sugar

5 garlic cloves, peeled and roughly chopped

1 tbsp Worcestershire sauce

2 tsp salt

2–3 jalapeño peppers or other hot chillies, roughly chopped

2 onions, peeled and roughly chopped

1 tsp chilli powder

1 tsp dried oregano

1 tsp dried thyme

1 tsp cornflour

1 tbsp white wine vinegar

1 tbsp vegetable oil

Place all the ingredients except the cornflour, vinegar and vegetable oil into the slow cooker dish and stir well.

Cover with the lid and cook on low for about 8 hours until the vegetables are very soft. Remove the lid and increase the temperature to high for the last hour of cooking.

Stir the cornflour into the vinegar to make a paste, then add it to the slow cooker dish together with the oil. Leave uncovered, stirring occasionally, for 20–30 minutes or until thickened.

Allow to cool, then pour the mixture into a food processor in batches and blitz until smooth. Pour into sterilised bottles, seal and store in the fridge for up to a month.

Onion and ale burger relish

PREPARATION TIME: 10 MINUTES

COOKING TIME: 5–7 HOURS

MAKES ABOUT 1KG (2¼LB)   VEGETARIAN

Perfect for burgers or equally good with bangers and mash.

1 tbsp olive oil

3 onions, peeled, halved and sliced

1 garlic clove, peeled and finely
  sliced

75g (3oz) dark soft brown sugar

Sea salt and freshly ground black
  pepper

2 red chillies, deseeded and finely
  chopped

1½ tbsp wholegrain mustard

250ml (9fl oz) ale

6 tbsp white wine vinegar

Place the olive oil, onions, garlic and 25g (1oz) of the sugar in the slow cooker dish. Season with salt and pepper, then cover with the lid and cook on high, stirring occasionally, for 2–3 hours or until the onions are caramelised and golden.

Add the remaining ingredients, then cook, uncovered, for 3–4 hours or until thick and almost all of the liquid has evaporated.

Allow to cool, then spoon into sterilised jars, seal and store in the fridge for up to three months.

WHAT ABOUT...

if you want to cook on the hob? Place in a non-reactive saucepan, cover with a lid and cook for 1 hour in step 1 and then for a further 30 minutes in step 2.

Tomato ketchup

PREPARATION TIME: 25 MINUTES

COOKING TIME: 6½–8½ HOURS PLUS COOLING

MAKES 1KG (2¼LB)   VEGETARIAN

Long, slow cooking suits tomatoes, drawing out all their flavour and sweetness; so for home-made ketchup slow cookers are perfect.

1.5kg (3lb 5oz) ripe tomatoes, roughly chopped

2 onions, peeled and sliced

½ large red pepper, deseeded and chopped

Sea salt and freshly ground black pepper

50g (2oz) soft brown sugar

100ml (3½fl oz) cider vinegar

1 tsp English mustard

1 cinnamon stick

1 tsp whole allspice

1 tsp whole cloves

1 tsp blade mace

1 tsp celery seeds

1 tsp black peppercorns

1 bay leaf

½ garlic clove

Paprika, to taste (optional)

3–4 heaped tsp cornflour

1–2 tbsp cold water

Combine the tomatoes, onion and chopped pepper in the slow cooker dish. Season well with salt and pepper, then cover with the lid and cook for 3–4 hours, stirring occasionally, until very soft. Remove and clean the cooker dish. Strain through a sieve using the back of a ladle to push as much through as possible. Return the mixture to the slow cooker dish. Add the sugar, vinegar and mustard.

Tie the cinnamon, allspice, cloves, mace, celery seeds, peppercorns, bay leaf and garlic in a square of muslin. Drop it into the mixture and cook, uncovered, on high for 3–4 hours, stirring occasionally until thickened.

Season to taste, adding paprika if you like. Mix the cornflour with enough cold water to form a paste, then add it to the mixture and stir well. Cook, uncovered, for a further 30 minutes or until thick and the mixture no longer tastes floury. Allow to cool. Remove the bag of spices, then pour the mixture through a funnel into sterilised bottles. Seal and store in the fridge for up to a month.

Eggnog

PREPARATION TIME: 10 MINUTES

COOKING TIME: 2–3 HOURS PLUS CHILLING

MAKES 1.2 LITRES (2 PINTS)   VEGETARIAN

Most eggnogs are made with raw egg but this is a cooked version for those who would rather not have raw egg, and is seriously yummy.

6 large eggs, separated

100g (3½oz) caster sugar, plus
  4 tbsp caster sugar

750ml (1¼ pints) whole milk

1 tsp vanilla extract

250ml (9fl oz) double cream

75ml (2½fl oz) brandy

75ml (2½fl oz) dark rum

A pinch of salt

¼ tsp freshly grated nutmeg, for
  sprinkling

Place the egg yolks, 100g (3½oz) of the sugar, milk and vanilla extract into a heatproof bowl that fits into your slow cooker dish.

Place the bowl in the slow cooker dish and carefully pour enough boiling water around the outside to come about halfway up the sides of the bowl. Cover with the lid and cook on high for 2–3 hours, whisking occasionally, until thickened.

Remove the bowl from the slow cooker dish and allow to cool slightly. Stir in the cream, brandy and rum.

To make the meringue, place the reserved egg whites, the 4 tablespoons of sugar and the salt in a heatproof mixing bowl and set over a saucepan of barely simmering water. Whisk with an electric mixer until thick and stiff peaks form.

Using a metal spoon, fold this meringue into the cooled yolk mixture until completely smooth and combined. Chill for at least 1 hour before serving in glasses, sprinkled with nutmeg.

Swedish glogg

PREPARATION TIME: 10 MINUTES

COOKING TIME: 2 HOURS

MAKES ABOUT 10–12 GLASSES   VEGETARIAN

Glogg is a hot, sweetened, mulled wine drunk in Sweden as a pre-dinner drink or as a warming afternoon pick-me-up. It is traditionally served in little cups or glasses with a spoon with which to eat the raisins and almonds.

75cl bottle good-quality red wine

1 orange, washed and dried

10 whole cloves

1 cinnamon sticks

10 cardamom pods, lightly crushed

200g (7oz) blanched almonds

200g (7oz) raisins

250g (9oz) caster sugar, or to taste

150ml (5fl oz) brandy

Pour the wine into the slow cooker dish.

Stud the orange with the cloves and add to the wine together with the cinnamon and cardamom. Cover with the lid and cook on high for 2 hours.

Stir in the almonds, raisins, sugar and brandy and cook, uncovered, for a further 30 minutes. Ladle into little cups or heatproof glasses to serve.

Hot winter Pimm's

PREPARATION TIME: 5 MINUTES

COOKING TIME: 2 HOURS

MAKES 10 GLASSES   VEGETARIAN

Not just for the summer, Pimm's is a great all-year-round drink, so try this winter variety in the colder months.

70cl bottle Pimm's Winter No. 3

2 litres (3½ pints) good-quality
  apple juice

12 whole cloves

1 cinnamon stick

1 whole nutmeg

2 pieces stem ginger

Place all the ingredients in the slow cooker dish.

Cover with the lid and cook on high for 2 hours.

Remove the spices with a slotted spoon and ladle into glasses to serve.

WHAT ABOUT...
if you want to cook conventionally? Warm the ingredients in a non-reactive, covered saucepan over a low heat for 2 hours and serve as above.

INDEX

Acknowledgements

Massive thanks to my editor, Lizzy Gray, who believed in me and gave me the chance to write this book – Lizzy, you're ace and have been so kind and supportive throughout, thank you. David, you've worked wonders with the photos in very little time – thank you. Thanks to Andy Boulton, beef buyer extraordinaire, for inspiring me to write a book on slow cooking in the first place, and for contributing such wonderful meat to work with. Thanks also to Frances Westerman, Aaron James and the team for the same, and to the farmers who lovingly produced it. Crock-Pot slow cookers must also be mentioned for their generous provision of slow cookers for recipe testing.

The biggest thanks of all go to my rocks: Mummy, Daddy, brother Simon and my gorgeous Rupert without whom I would achieve very little. Oh, and thanks to Long-legs, Buzz and SSN who didn't think they'd get a mention.